WHERE DOES IT HURT NOW?

STERLING HAYNES
MD

Sterling Haynes

randArt Publishing
Email: zacharias.rand@gmail.com

Cover by Charlotte Falk
http://www.charlottefalk.ca

Edited by Rand Zacharias

Chilcotin photos thankfully donated from the Sage Birchwater collection. Personal photos are from the Haynes family collections.

Library and Archives Canada Cataloguing in Publication

Haynes, Sterling
       Where Does It Hurt Now?

ISBN-13: 978-1499139006

ISBN-10: 1499139004

I dedicate my book to the women in my life.

Our eldest daughter, Elizabeth Jane Haynes, got me started writing in retirement and was a driving force in editing and promoting my work. Elizabeth is a great writer and she has taken time from her job and her writing to be my mentor along my writing path.

My loving family, starting with my beloved Jessie, and our three younger daughters—Melissa, Jocelyn and Leslie—have also always been supportive of my poetry and stories. Leslie has been superb with pointed, well-chosen remarks and revisions of my written words.

My parents made me who I was and am in this life—my mother, Elizabeth Sterling Haynes, and my father, Nelson Willard Haynes.

Sterling Haynes

Table of Contents

Sterling Haynes

Introduction

Laughter has been a big part of my life. A belly laugh can put things into perspective. A chuckle can give me a different slant and a way to turn to find the solution or make a difficult diagnosis.

When I started into practice there were no machines to make a diagnosis or computers to find the solution, especially in a rural setting. It seems odd now but the general practitioner used to talk to the patients and by history taking and the physical examination come to a reasonable conclusion. Later, this method helped me make a more accurate diagnosis when I learned which machine to use and where to point it. Compassion and good humour set up the bond between the patient and the doctor. I am not sure that the ten-minute doctor visit and the limitation of the client to only one problem is the way to approach medicine's complexities.

When I returned to Canada from northern Nigeria, after being stationed as a colonial officer on the south edge of the Sahara for three years, my ideas were altruistic. I kept with me visions of Hausa and Fulani people and their hump-backed cattle dying of starvation at the side of the road.

Another image was that of a silent village of over five hundred souls along the Benue River. All were dying or dead from African sleeping sickness. Overhead were hundreds of vultures circling above waiting for their feast.

When I enrolled in medical school at the University of Alberta in 1954, medicine, for me, was a calling not a business. There was no Medicare, no large salaries and, in fact, most doctors were poor, but compassionate. My sister Shirley and I practised medicine for almost a hundred years between us. We raised and educated our children, but the bottom line was not what we were interested in. We provided a service. I delivered about three thousand babies and that was my fulfillment. I would not have missed it for the world.

Now, in my 86th year I want to seize each day. I want to live each day to the fullest.

I want to end this introduction with my poem. *Carpe Diem* was a poem by Horace, from his Odes. He inspired me to write:

Seize the Day

Light is sweet,
it shines on my retina,
confronts my demons.
Soon I'll break out of my box—
be a person of the moment
in my bright sun.
Melancholy's shadows
are no longer
focused. In the
shiny reflections, I
enjoy hope and exuberance.
Let them go, let them go...
the black dogs of doom.
The joys of today blanket
the troubles of tomorrow.
Laugh and seize the day.

Family

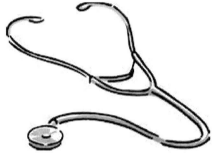

Compassion

My mother and father were very compassionate people. They were very generous with their skills and their money, especially during the years of what we, on this planet, called The Great Depression.

They lived in the province of Alberta, Canada at the time. Mother's younger brother, Wallace Sterling, had just graduated from the University of Toronto with a bachelor of arts degree in history. While at University of Toronto, he had been the mainstay star of the Toronto University Blues football team. When he graduated in 1927, there were very few jobs in Canada available to him and he went west to Edmonton with experience on the gridiron and a degree in the arts.

With the help of their friend, history professor George Hardy at the University of Alberta, they arranged for Wally to coach the university's Golden Bears football team and take graduate work in history from 1928 to 1930. Wally received his master's degree in 1930 and the Golden Bears did well under his leadership. The team won the conference title in 1928.

Uncle Wally stayed at our house while he was in Edmonton and I can vaguely remember him babysitting me and playing with me during his busy life in Alberta. Mother and Dad supported him during those lean years.

In 1930, Wally went to Stanford University to pursue his doctorate. He left Canada for good.

While at Stanford, he got a job as research assistant at the Hoover Library. He augmented his income by teaching in the history department. During his time at Stanford, he also tutored teenagers in English and history, enabling them to pass their final high school examinations. While tutoring, he was hired by Robert Millikan, Nobel Prize winner in physics, to teach his three sons. With all his part-time jobs, he soon had enough money to complete his PhD in 1938. Upon graduation, he joined the teaching staff of the California Institute of Technology where Robert Millikan was a prominent teacher and researcher. Wally was elected chairman of the faculty in 1944.

From 1944 to 1946, Wally was a part-time evening news commentator for CBS in Los Angeles. In Edmonton, we always made an effort to listen to the six o'clock news and Wally's take on the Allies victories and defeats during World War II. He was terrific and being a trained historian, always put his slant on the news.

In 1949, Wally was appointed as the director of the Huntington Library and Art Gallery. This lasted for a short-lived span of five months, as he later accepted the presidency of Stanford University. Wally was president for 19 years and made Stanford one of the leading universities in the world. He was the man with the Midas touch and while he held the position, the endowments nearly doubled. The faculty size almost tripled under his leadership, graduate school programs were improved and major building plans approved.

The medical school was moved from San Francisco to the campus and the Stanford linear accelerator was built. In 1968, he retired from the university as its president, but stayed on as chancellor for life. Wally died on Canada Day, July 1, 1985.

Sterling Haynes

During the 1930's, my folks established a warm place for the homeless workers who flocked to Edmonton. Wally had left for California and his basement room was empty for those in need.

The city of Edmonton was paying men to shovel snow from the streets at the rate of five cents an hour. They could also receive seven cents an hour to shovel sand and salt from the back of a truck onto Edmonton's slippery roads. Unfortunately, some of these men had no warm homes in which to sleep and they were always hungry from shovelling ten hours a day, six days a week.

Mother served dinner to all the men who came to our door, two at a time, hungry in the winter. They were given food and a place to sleep, but after breakfast they had to leave the house by eight o'clock in the morning. Supper for each consisted of six eggs, pickled pigs' feet, sauerkraut, bread, butter, jam, tea and half a pie. Breakfast was the same, but the pie was omitted and coffee added.

My father was a dentist and as money was in short supply, Dad was paid with pickled pigs' hocks, eggs preserved in water glass jars and crocks of sauerkraut. We had food galore.

I was kept busy along with my sister, Shirley, helping mother with clean up and dishes. Mother looked after these men until the economy started to improve between the years of 1935 and 1937 and the men stopped coming.
.

Mother was very busy as she started to work for the University of Alberta's department of extension after she co-founded the Banff School of Fine Arts in 1933.

A long time visitor to our house in the Garneau district was Alex Makravich during the 1920's and 30's. In Edmonton, it was common to have chicken every Sunday at two o'clock in the afternoon, usually after church. Alex was always invited and would tell us his World War I stories with great zeal. Sometimes, it was hard to follow the plots due to Alex's Russian accent and his dislike for Germans.

Alex cooked breakfast for the young co-eds in the Pembina residence at the University of Alberta for many years. Alex sometimes argued with his boss, Adolph Schultz, the chief cook. We always heard about what Schultz was up to—along with a description of his German cuisine and temperament. Alex never seemed to tire of the breakfast menu or the hours of work preparing breakfast for these vivacious young women students.

Alex was a great friend of my parents, Nelson and Elizabeth, and he was devoted to them. He could fix most things and was a great shoveller of snow for our sidewalk and driveway. His cooking was one of his many accomplishments but he always relished chicken dinners at our place. During the winter, he would turn up to shovel snow around our house or shovel coal into our furnace room. In May, he dug our garden in readiness for planting.

As a young man, Alex became a soldier and served under Tsar Nicholas II. He fought with the Russians against Germany from 1914 to 1917. When the Russian tsar was forced to abdicate on March 1st, 1917—Alex was out of work.

He became a mercenary for the Allies and signed on as a Belgian machine gunner. Because he couldn't speak Flemish and he had a Scottish-sounding name, his Belgian commander had him transferred to the Black Watch Regiment. The Scots couldn't understand him so they transferred him to Winnipeg's Cameron Highlander Regiment, where there were Russian-speaking Canadian soldiers.

In 1918, Alex was discharged from the army in Toronto and he had no place to go. The United Church of Canada sponsored him. When they couldn't find him a job in the Toronto area, they sent him to Chatham to help my grandfather, Reverend William Sterling, as a church handyman. Alex was provided with a room in the United Church manse.

I remember Mother telling me that Alex arrived in the dead of winter and was dressed in battle dress, but his kilt didn't protect his legs in 40 below temperatures. He arrived about suppertime, cold and hungry. Alex ate for about an hour and for dessert, Mother gave him a dish of preserved unpitted plums. After he finished the plums his cheeks were bulging. Before Mother could supply a bowl for the pits, Alex sprayed the pits all over the floor.

Mother knew then that she had to help this man-soldier become a Canadian. Mother, in her spare time, taught Alex to read and write English and to speak well despite a Russian accent. With my grandfather and grandmother providing the knowledge and decorum of the Victorian upper crust, Alex's table manners became exemplary. His work as a handyman was excellent and he soon became a good cook for the family.

My mother and father were married four years after the Great War ended, and in 1923 they moved to Edmonton. Alex missed my mother and became melancholy. He had liked her dedication to teaching him English, history and literature. On a cold winter day in 1923, Alex appeared without warning, at my parents' doorstep, in Edmonton. He was hungry and cold. He had quit his job at the manse and followed my mother west.

Alex was welcomed and given the spare bedroom in the basement until Mother found Alex a job at the University of

Alberta as a cook. He cooked breakfast at Pembina Hall, a woman's residence on campus, for over 30 years.

Alex was a permanent fixture at our Sunday dinners until he died. We all mourned him and missed his exuberant war stories and his caring nature. Sunday dinners never seemed to be the same after he was gone.

My mother and father had many theatre friends. Mostly, they were poor actors who needed help during the Depression. My folks offered to share what they had with this talented group. Mother was active in Edmonton's Little Theatre and a dramatist at the University of Alberta.

Geoffrey came to our house in the winter of 1931. He was a well-educated, unemployed English actor trying to survive in the cold environs of the province of Alberta.

Geoffrey had knocked about in western Canada for a few years, carrying two leather suitcases fastened with brown belts. Strapped to his suitcase were a cricket bat and a tennis racquet. Geoffrey was a remittance man from England's upper crust, when the remittance of money from nobility stopped suddenly during the Great Depression.

Geoff had a sense of class and a great deal of panache. He had great stage presence, a marvellous speaking voice and joined the Edmonton Little Theatre. When the leading man in the latest play developed laryngitis, Geoff filled in with skill and alacrity. He fit the part and his handsome profile, accent and enunciation fit Noel Coward's drawing room comedy. He was a natural thespian.

After rehearsal one January night, it was discovered that Geoffrey had no place to stay. My mother, Elizabeth, the director of the play, took Geoffrey under her wing and brought him home. He stayed in our home off and on for almost four years. Usually, he slept on the couch in the living room and occasionally on the cot in the furnace room.

Geoffrey was an immaculate dresser. He still possessed his tweed suits and plus fours—baggy pants used for sporting activities with fastened four-inch folds beneath the knees. His shirts had detachable collars with collar buttons and his shirt cuffs closed with cuff links emblazoned with the family crest. He liked to wear an English rose in his lapel, when he was in the money, but he never thought he was a thorn in the side of the Empire, the United Kingdom. He was always on the lookout for women with money.

Finally, Mother found him a part-time job with the University of Alberta radio station, CKUA. Geoffrey's mellifluous voice and English accent *wowed* the Edmontonians. After a few months, he was hired as a full-time radio announcer in Grand Prairie, Alberta. On holidays and long weekends, he often came for visits to Edmonton.

At about this time, my mother had employed a live-in babysitter named May. Mother forgot to tell May about Geoffrey's arrival. On the day before Christmas, Geoffrey arrived during a winter snowstorm at about midnight. He had taken the streetcar from the Canadian National Railroad station to our house. He plunked his bags in the hall and stretched out on the sofa with his coat covering him. His snores awakened May.

She crept down the stairs and onto the front porch, unstrapped Geoffrey's cricket bat from his suitcase, and crept up to the sleeping man. May clobbered the apparent intruder on the face and forehead with the bat.

16

"My God, you've broken my nose," shouted Geoffrey. We all heard the commotion and ran downstairs. My father grabbed a towel and staunched the flow of blood before it stained the new Chesterfield.

Dad spent Christmas Day repairing Geoffrey's teeth and broken nose. A few days later, Geoffrey announced that he was feeling better and the bruising was subsiding. He did complain that he had missed his Christmas dinner of turkey with all the trimmings. With my dad's help, Geoffrey bought a one-way train ticket to Toronto.

A few months later, we received a letter from him with a cheque for 50 dollars and a thank you for four warm years. He was working as a radio announcer for the CBC in Toronto and had met a wealthy woman of the horsey set. He was looking forward to a life of polo, cricket, theatre, Scotch whisky and marital bliss. The letter was signed, "With love, Geoffrey."

A shot of Edmonton's Studio Theatre in 1945.

17

Elizabeth Sterling Haynes plays the mad woman in Jean Giraudoux's play, The Mad Woman of Chaillot, *circa 1950. It took place inside the Quonset hut theatre studio.*

Another shot of the mad woman from the 1950's performance.

Emeritus professor of drama Tom Peacocke wrote about his favourite teacher Elizabeth Sterling Haynes in 1952 when he was a young theatre student at the University of Alberta. He was involved in the production of *The Mad Woman of Chaillot* to a minor degree.

What in God's name am I doing here," I thought. "I'm only in this bloody course because I can neither draw, nor paint nor sing nor play an instrument. I'm no good with tools, it's hot up here, the bolt won't turn, and who the hell are these creeps in drama, anyway?

During a quiet moment, a voice the like of which I had never heard before floated through the auditorium...rich, resonant and vital.

I remember striving to imagine what body, what face, could produce such a sound. Purposely, I dropped my wrench to the floor and climbed down to retrieve it. I fixed my gaze on the most statuesque figure I had ever seen. It was at that moment that I subconsciously began to reconsider the direction my life would take.

There was nothing in our working relationship from then until she died that was not a source of inspiration to me. As I write this, Beethoven's Ninth is playing in the background. A happy accident, for the work of Elizabeth Sterling Haynes seems to me, upon reflection, always to have been a 'Hymn of Joy.'

Tom Peacocke

Sterling's father, Sergeant Nelson W. Haynes, in World War I uniform.

Dad

My dad was given his namesake after the famed Englishman Lord Nelson, but his friends on the baseball field, the soccer field and at the YMCA gym called him Boss Haynes and sometimes Nellie. When Boss was 16, his older brother, Fred, and his many cousins played baseball for Fullarton Corners, a town in Ontario. In 1916, this was a true farm team from the sticks.

Surprisingly, these young men won the Ontario senior baseball championship, defeating Toronto in the final five-game playoff. His cousin, George Baker, a huge Ontario farm kid, pitched all five championship games, even the double headers. Wags said "that the baker had a rising fastball."

Dad played shortstop and his older brother Fred was the catcher. Baker was the captain but Boss Haynes ran the team after the farm chores were all completed. Boss was a smart, tough, redhead—a guy who batted left and threw right-handed. He was good with the glove and a great bunter. My future father was 16 years of age, it was to be his last season with the Fullarton Corners Giants. He couldn't hit worth a damn but was a good shortstop. He could turn the double play with the best of players. The inside of both his legs were scarred by spike marks made by aggressive base runners.

In September, after the Ontario Little World Series, he went to the University of Toronto and registered as a dental student. At the end of his first university term, in 1916, he enlisted in the Canadian Army Expeditionary Forces. He'd just turned 17. During boot camp, at Aldershot in the Maritimes, he learned to shoot a sniper's gun, the Ross rifle, and how to use explosives.

When he arrived overseas, he was transferred to the Dental Corps—a branch of the Expeditionary Forces and he soon learned to do general dentistry, although unqualified. At tent camp in Aldershot, England, he learned to handle all dental, facial wounds and fractures received by soldiers while on the front lines of the war, including the wounded from the battle of Vimy Ridge in France. Their operating theatre was a massive tent in the Canadian Army's tent city.

Early in 1918, Boss was promoted to sergeant. While in England, he learned to become a very good soccer player, an extremely gifted dental surgeon and to save his money. He knew dental school could be expensive, but as a sergeant he made a dollar a day. He saved every penny. Soon he had almost enough money to finance his dental studies when he returned to Canada. After the armistice in 1918, he was discharged from the army and began dental school at the University of Toronto.

In the summers, between dental school semesters, Boss worked hard clearing land in Alberta. He was tough as a ploughshare and worked with a double-bitted axe, a grub hook, dynamite and a team of horses. He batched by himself in a tent by the smouldering tree stumps. The smoke, he said, "kept the mosquitoes and black flies away." Alone, he cleared two Alberta farms: 160 acres at Killam and the same size of acreage at Irma. At the end of each summer in the sun, he was orange from a mass of freckles and peeling skin. Physically, at the end of the summer, he was as hard as a spruce knot.

I remember Dad told me that he saw new Ukrainian immigrants using breaking ploughs to farm and sow crops from the unbroken land. These ploughs were pulled by teams of eight Amazonian-like women.

Dad was in great demand—he played ball for the local town teams in Sunday afternoon doubleheaders. He always lent a hand to his Russian farm friends, usually after Sunday games. Boss used dynamite sticks to blow up stumps for his local neighbours. He had learned to use TNT as a young World War I army recruit. He was as explosive on the ball field as he was around stumps and massive rocks that occupied most Alberta homesteads.

In dental school, he was a standout. He had practiced dental procedures as a non-commissioned officer in the army and studied human anatomy of the head and neck in his spare time. Apart from playing soccer for the Toronto University Blues, he had little recreation and very little money. He was a good student. He graduated in 1922 with a DDS, or a degree in dental surgery.

Soon after he married my mother, Elizabeth Sterling, the eldest daughter of Annie and Will Sterling, a United Church preacher. Elizabeth and Nelson had been sweethearts in high school at Stratford Collegiate and attended the university together.

When Dad received his degree, he and Elizabeth moved to Carleton Place, Ontario. He was very popular, in charge of a thriving practice, and was elected mayor of the town for a year. They then decided to move west and perhaps practice dentistry in Alberta with his oldest brother Wesley. This plan never worked out as Mother didn't want to move to a small town in Alberta.

After they moved to the larger metropolis of Edmonton, Dad set up a dental practice at 214 Empire Building on the corner of 101 Street and Jasper Avenue. He was busy in Edmonton, but for three days every two weeks, he packed up his portable chair and professional equipment to visit farming communities on the Canadian National Railroad to practice dentistry–Hughendon, Hardisty, Provost, Metiskow, and sometimes Lloydminster.

His office was in his hotel room and he did general dentistry under adverse conditions: He cared for fractured jaws, impacted teeth and full teeth extractions. All the farmers were early risers and his clients were at his hotel room at dawn waiting for treatment. Dad could see he needed more training so enrolled in a post-graduate course in Chicago, successfully completing his MDS, master's degree of dental surgery.

He was the first super specialist in Alberta to look after broken mandibles and maxillae as well as impacted wisdom teeth. He reduced all fractures, applied arch wire splints for broken lower jaws and wired Lefort complicated fractures of the maxilla along with other facial fractures.

Sometimes he had to make special dental plates for farmers with no teeth, wiring their jaws shut for healing using the new splints. Farmers at this time were at risk at work. They could be kicked in the jaw by unruly horses or battered by kickbacks while starting Ford model-T cars or balky tractors. If the steel cranks backfired and hit the drivers in the jaw, bones were broken.

As his practice grew, Dad bought an X-ray unit for his office to check for facial fractures and his post-reduction fracture results. This primitive machine scattered cathode rays and caused radiation dermatitis to my father's hands in a few years—eventually causing him to acquire lymphocytic leukemia from the wide scatter of the gamma rays.

Dad was busy nights from seven to eleven o'clock when he did most of his operative dentistry—which included impacted wisdom teeth and broken jaws. It was the days before antibiotics and endotracheal general anaesthesia. Instead, during these early days of modern medicine, dentists used local procaine blocks with intermittent shots of morphine. All dental tools were sterilized with the use of steam and care was taken to have aseptic fields for this type of surgery.

When I was a high school student during the 1940s, Dad elected me to become his first assistant, at night, in his downtown office. A badly broken mandible was easily fixed when the jaw was wired shut and secured with arch wire splints and rubber bands. A maxilla fracture could take up to three hours to reduce and fix with a stainless steel wire—longer if the wire broke during the fixation of the fracture. Dad was very good at doing the nerve blocks with procaine and then immobilizing the fractures with splints and wires. Everything was checked with his office X-rays and fluoroscopy until the bones were in their correct anatomical position. The dexterity and strength needed to do this resulted in the development of my dad's powerful hands. It was during these times that my father taught me the surgical anatomy of the head and neck. A few years later, this knowledge would help me study this subject at the University of Alberta's medical school.

Dad's finished surgical results were very good. When endotracheal anaesthesia became available in the Misericordia and Royal Alexander Hospitals in Edmonton, the more difficult cases were moved there. Before the era of controlled ether, or laughing gas (nitrous oxide) by endotracheal administration, local injections were used with intermittent bouts of morphine injected intramuscularly. This injection gave the patient relief from long surgical procedures in his office's dental chair. At the end of long procedures, both the patient and Dad had to lie down from the exhaustive surgery. My job was to clean up and sterilize all the surgical instruments. I had to make sure the patients were driven home or taken back to their hotel if they were from out of town.

Dad was compassionate and concerned for the welfare of kids and their parents on the dole. His Saturday mornings were spent looking after children's teeth and those of adults in the afternoon. He gave of his time and his skills freely. The city of Edmonton's welfare department kept him over-booked with emergency dentistry.

When Dad died in 1958 from lymphatic leukemia, I found his safety deposit box full of useless Alberta Prosperity certificates in one dollar denominations. This so-called "funny money" was produced by Premier Bill Aberhart and his Social Credit government in 1936. The Supreme Court of Canada declared this funny money to be illegal tender by 1938. The hundreds of useless dollar bills were supposed to have paid for the difficult surgery my father had done during the Depression years in Alberta.

Dad's early death from leukemia, at age fifty-nine, was attributed to the long-term effects of scattered gamma rays from his early X-ray machines. He used to check the reduction of facial fractures without wearing lead shields for protection. The chronic exfoliative dermatitis of his hands, which caused his skin to weep constantly, was due to scattered X-ray radiation exposure from the primitive machines. He would use his hands to hold the *wing bite* X-ray films to each patient's mouth.

When I checked his office contents, after his funeral in Clinton, Ontario, I found his sniper's gun from the army, a Ross rifle wrapped in oily rags. I stuffed the funny money in the bank's garbage bin—my father's services were their own reward—and mine.

Elizabeth Sterling Haynes in the photograph used for the cover portrait.

Mother's Rebirth

December 7, 1941 lives on in my memory. Even though I was only 14 years old, I distinctly remember what happened to *my* family that day.

It was two o'clock in the afternoon and I was skating with the Sawatsky twins and my best friend, Percy, at the Garneau Community rink in Edmonton. Blaring out of the arena speakers was the song, "I've got a Lovely Bunch of Coconuts." Halfway through, the music stopped and an announcer said, "The United States has declared war on Japan. The American naval and marine casualties at Pearl Harbor are large and many war ships were destroyed." Then the music came back on and everyone resumed skating.

Soon after, my dad appeared outside the fence of the skating rink. His face was ashen, his lips set tight. I just knew in that moment something was wrong and it wasn't the news of war. It had to be about my mother.

"Sterling, change your skates right away. Mother is really sick. You have to transfuse your mother with your blood. We need at least a quart of blood from you and another quart from Shirley."

At age 43, my mother had developed cancer of the womb and received preoperative radium inserts to contain her malignancy. On the previous Friday, she underwent a hysterectomy and lost a significant amount of blood. However, surgeon-gynaecologist Dr. Horner found that she was bleeding again and would need two massive blood transfusions.

Dad had taken the car out of the garage and parked on 84th Avenue in front of our house. Shirley was already sitting in the front seat. The tires crunched through snow and ice as Dad drove the four blocks to the university's hospital.

Dr. Horner was waiting at the top steps of the hospital. He rushed us into a small operating room theatre that was divided by a raised six-foot stage. It contained a stretcher, numerous lengths of glass partitions and a long piece of rubber tubing. I climbed the stairs to the raised platform. As I shed my warm clothes and peeled down my long winter underwear, the doctor instructed me to lie on the stretcher. Mother lay pale and motionless on a stretcher below me.

"Dad, is Mom okay? She'll be okay, Dr. Horner? Won't she?"

"Yes, son, she'll be okay once she gets your blood into her. You pay strict attention to what Dr. Horner tells you," said Dad.

"Sterling, I am going to put a large needle into your arm and we are going to run blood from your arm to your mother's arm. Your mother is very tired now, but as soon as the blood is given, she will perk up a bit. The blood will flow by gravity. You must lie still for about an hour, you understand?" said Dr. Horner.

"Yes sir, I understand, I won't move a muscle. I'm pretty tough. Hope Mom will be okay soon."

The blood started to flow down the rubber tubing like it was a massive umbilical cord.

After about an hour, Mother seemed a little more restless and spoke to me.

"Are you all right, Sterling? You know, I seem to feel better already," she said in a low, husky voice.

"Yeah, I'm okay, Mom. I've got lots of blood. I'm a big, strong kid. When I'm finished here, Shirley is waiting to come in and give you more blood."

My eyes widened as I looked down at my pale mother. The red lifeline tubing was prominent against the white sheets and her arm.

Mother was sobbing.

Shirley came in and lay on the stretcher where I had been. Dr. Horner disconnected the needle from my arm and hooked the long rubber tubing to a new needle in my sister's arm. I was a bit lightheaded at first. Dr. Horner told me I'd given my mother over two pints of blood, but I could still go back to school the next day.

My dad and sister stayed with our matriarch at the hospital. Dad told me to walk home and get supper ready. They'd be back around seven o'clock that evening.

"Your mom will be fine now. Your Group O, Rh positive blood was a great birthday present to her," said Dr. Horner.

Yes, ironically, December 7, 1941 was my mother's 44th birthday.

I remember walking back home along the roadway at dusk. People were putting their house lights on and the bulbs cast a yellow glow, creating long fingers of shadow. I kicked the large frozen droppings left from the horses that pulled bread wagons and milk carts. I knew Mom would be better now with our new blood and would soon be home from the hospital.

This is Sterling at the approximate time of his mother's need for blood...he is 14 or 15 years of age in this photograph.

I started to sing and dance as I walked along the icy, snow-covered road, "I've got a lovely bunch of coconuts, big ones, thick ones, some as big as your head."

our mother was reborn as a teacher, dramatist and writer. She
taught drama in the University of Alberta's drama department and
Edmonton's unique Studio Theatre. She inspired student actors and
actresses, and established drama as an elective subject for the
Alberta high school curriculum.

Today, her legacy to the city of Edmonton's theatre has
been established, in perpetuity, by the Sterling Awards given
yearly to the best actors, playwrights, directors, producers and
drama teachers in Alberta.

In 1950, our mother wrote:

*The door of the Studio Theatre opened and a girl came
in...young and eager, walking as if, already, she saw her name in
lights. I had never actually seen that girl before—and yet I had
seen her many times, in many hopeful faces. To me she is always
Miss Alberta, dreaming of becoming an actress.*

Sterling Haynes

"Shirl"

In memory of Shirley (Haynes) Appleby MD (University of Alberta, class of 1948)

Consider this as a biography of Shirl from the perspective of a somewhat doltish, but doting, younger brother.

My sister was a strong, compassionate woman with a great intellect. Shirley was a Latin scholar and a physics whiz. She took time to tutor a neighbourhood kid from down the street, Jimmy Stollery, and me in both subjects. Thanks to her, we handily passed our university entrance examinations. Jimmy took engineering, going on to own a large construction firm. Later, he was a philanthropist—his firm recently opened the Stollery Children's Hospital in Edmonton. Shirley's influence was strong and abiding.

Shirley was physically strong—she might have said, strong as a horse. As a teenager, she became an accomplished equestrian. She used an English saddle, don't you know, at the Greening School of Horsemanship in Edmonton's Garneau area. Mrs. Greening was an English taskmistress and Shirley rose to the occasion, becoming a sophisticated, elegant rider.

Shirley was a good ping-pong player, too, and won local tournaments with her fabulous forehand smash. Shirl could take me in arm wrestling until I was 14.

From an early age, her compassion for all living things was legendary. Her first two dogs were Sealyham Terriers. Rags and Tatters were her good friends. And the dogs she owned over the years are too numerous to name. The connection with animals

34

continued her whole life. She was a card-carrying member of the Society for the Prevention of Cruelty to Animals.

Intellectually and academically, Shirl was the tops—the absolute tops. In the ninth grade, she won the Lt. Governor's Gold Medal for the highest marks in New Brunswick's high school entrance examinations; we lived in the eastern province for a year. She had the highest marks in the University of Alberta's entrance examination and won the prestigious Tegler Scholarship along with three other bursaries. These paid her university fees at the University of Alberta for four years. In 2011, when we were speaking on the phone, she said, "I just wanted you to know that my education didn't cost anybody anything." Of that, she was rightly proud.

Shirl was a true Canadian, very patriotic. Two of her male admirers during World War II were Sergeant Manoz Greening, who was killed at the age of 21 in the Italian Campaign and Flight Sergeant Fraser Hollemback, a bombardier who was shot down over the North Sea and drowned. Fraser was 20 when he died. After those tragic deaths, with the war still raging, Shirl felt an obligation to serve her country.

After her second year at medical school, in 1944, Shirley joined the Canadian Army. She was stationed in the army hospital in Dundurn, Saskatchewan, where she was in charge of the X-ray unit. She remained there until the war ended.

After the war, she finished her medical studies under the auspices of the Canadian Army and received her licence to practise as a doctor in 1948. The army paid for her complete medical education.

Soon a Yorkshire man-cum-Victorian, John Appleby, a fellow medical student, became a permanent fixture at our house in Edmonton. For Shirl's romantic evenings with John, she would play the record *For Thee Alone—ad nauseum*, to my tender ears— sung by her favourite Metropolitan Opera tenor, Richard Crooks. As her cheeky brother and short order cook in the kitchen, I always made sure my smart remarks could be heard by them as they cuddled on the couch in the living room.

On the last day of their final exams—that very afternoon— Shirley and John were married by the Justice of the Peace in Edmonton's city hall. It was a very casual wedding, as Shirley was not very big on ceremony. My mother, the ultimate dramatist, loved John dearly, but was none too happy about the austerity and lack of ambiance enveloping their city hall wedding ceremony.

This was Shirley—sure of her way and eager for the next adventure.

After her internship at the Royal Alexandra Hospital in Edmonton, Shirley and John took further training at the rural Ponoka Mental Hospital and then Rhode Island, where they both were chosen for highly-sought after residencies.

It was in Providence, Rhode Island that their first child, Margaret, was born. Afterwards, Shirl completed three years of neurological training in Denver, at the Colorado General Hospital. Soon after their move to Denver, Johnny, and then the twins, Barbara and Mary, were born. Despite giving birth to so many babies and studying hard, Shirl never missed a day of work or training. She was one tough woman and a very loving mother.

After acquiring certification in their specialities, John and Shirley moved to Toronto and worked at the Scarborough General Hospital. Medicine and their family took up all of their time.

Sarah, Jennifer and Alice were born in Toronto. I was blessed with more and more nieces! Life was hectic and their work was demanding.

In 1969, wanting a change, they sold their house and took all the kids on a four-month tour through Europe. While they were in Italy, an innkeeper looked at Shirl and John and counted loudly as each of the seven kids entered the cafe behind their parents—he then jumped to his feet and shouted, "Bravo, Bravo," clapping John on the back.

When the family returned to Canada, they settled and stayed in Prescott, Ontario. John became the chief psychiatrist at the Brockville Psychiatric Hospital, as well, they both worked across the St. Lawrence River in the Ogdensburg Psychiatric Hospital in New York.

Later, Shirl opened her own office and practised family medicine in Prescott. She gave new meaning to the phrase, "devoted doctor." She was county coroner for many years and knew every Ontario provincial police officer between Kingston and Cornwall along Highway 401. Her coroner's work, at times, involved investigating motor vehicle accident fatalities.

I was so very proud of my sister. She practised medicine for 60 years. Can you imagine being on call every third or fourth night for 60 years? Together we practised medicine for almost 100 years, but never in the same place.

Sterling Haynes

Thank God, because I could never have kept up with my sister. Throughout our lives, Shirley remained my best teacher and favourite mentor.

Shirley passed away in Kingston on November 3, 2011—after a lengthy illness. Shirley's legacy to the world lives in her seven children, 15 grandchildren and her immensely large extended family of patients, friends and fans.

Her life was lived, with no remorse and by her code of ethics: compassion, love, honesty and fair play.

I miss her.

Teddy

In 1932, Ned Corbett, Ted Cohen and Elizabeth Sterling Haynes became founding members of the Banff School of Fine Arts in Alberta. This school has international recognition today. The first summer school took place in the Banff Elementary School on Banff Avenue. This trio expected ten students but over 120 registered. The cost was one dollar for the six-week course and mostly attracted Alberta teachers and university students. Ted taught many courses in stagecraft, stage design, creative writing and puppeteering. His days were full and the first summer school was a great success despite the shortage of fine arts teachers. The small mountain town was overwhelmed, but the Banff School district opened the local schools as dormitories and allowed tent camps on the school grounds.

Teddy Cohen was a small handsome man with impeccable manners. He had a black pencil-thin moustache and olive skin. His black hair was always controlled in a pompadour. His dress was casual but he often wore a tweed jacket with light-coloured gabardine pants. His pants were always pressed with a knife edge crease; his shoes were always shined and he wore a snap brim fedora, always well-blocked. Teddy dressed the part of a lawyer, but people were surprised when they learned he was a puppeteer, teacher, writer and dramatist. The only thing that marred Ted's appearance was the fact that he was a chain smoker, so he always had a cigarette between his fingers or in his mouth.

In 1933, the three founding members of the Banff School of Fine Arts lobbied the Carnegie Foundation in the U.S. to donate $10,000 to build a small stone theatre on Banff Avenue. Teddy had graduated in law from the University of Alberta in 1930 and used his legal expertise to seal the deal. After Teddy became involved with the school, he seldom practiced law again.

Teddy was born on May 8, 1908 in Winnipeg. His parents, David and Katie, were from Lithuania and were in search of freedom and opportunity in Canada. They were nomads and David was a pedlar. In 1907, Katie and her daughters, Lilly and Jessie, docked in Halifax and took the train across the eastern half of Canada to Winnipeg to join David. On that windswept platform in a blizzard, Katie was disappointed. "We left Gan Eden (the Garden of Eden) for this desolate place?" she reportedly cried. Their second child, Jessie, always remembered swooping down to grab a handful of the white stuff on the station platform. "Mamma, Mamma, sugar," she said. She let out a wail as the snow touched her lips.[1]

The following year David and his brother, Morris, peddled their wares to the farmers of Saskatchewan and Manitoba. Katie stayed in Winnipeg. In 1908, Teddy, their first son, was born. Soon after, Katie and the family joined David in Smoky Lake, Alberta. They moved on to Vancouver by land and by boat to Prince Rupert, where a second son, Eliot, was born on June 19, 1912. It was a sad day because Lilly, the eldest daughter, died of quinsy, a peritonsillar abscess, the same day that Eliot was born.[2]

The family increased by two in Alberta when Hazel was born in 1915 and Hymie in 1917. Now with four children, Dave and Katie opened a series of ladies' ready-to-wear stores in Edmonton so Teddy could go to good schools and then university.

---

[1] Taken from the article *David Cohen, The Wandering Jew* by Myra Paperney in the magazine *Heritage*, Volume 3 Number 2 Fall 2001, page 3.

[2] Taken from the same article also on page 3 by Myra Paperney.

Ted would take law, as I mentioned earlier, and later, Eliot would take engineering and medicine at the University of Alberta. Their nomadic spirit then drove the parents to migrate to Palestine in the mid 1930's. They left the full-grown offspring at home in Alberta. I remember Dave telling me, "They only stayed in Palestine for a year because they didn't like speaking Hebrew and the main language spoken in the market place was Arabic."

When Katie and Dave returned to Alberta from Palestine, they opened the Hay Lake Mercantile, a country general store that sold gasoline, horse harnesses, groceries and dry goods. There was no running water and often no electricity. The couple lived on the upper floor of the store. It was up to Teddy and Eliot to do the store's books and keep David out of financial trouble.

As a kid in those Depression years, I got to know Teddy well. He was often at the house discussing plays, production and his latest puppet show in Edmonton with my folks. He always had a piece of soft pine in his jacket pocket, and with a series of knives, fine chisels, gouges and sandpaper, he was constantly working on the heads of his 18-string marionettes. In the winters of 1933 and 1934, there were two Saturday matinee performances of puppet plays held in a warehouse at 106 Street just off Jasper Avenue in Edmonton. My buddies and I always went. For a nickel we had a great time. Each of Teddy's productions was a masterpiece of design, creative writing, stagecraft and performance.

For my seventh birthday, Teddy bought me a baseball glove. It was made from soft leather and was a shortstop's glove—my dad played shortstop for the Edmonton Arrow's baseball team. I was determined to be a shortstop. I began playing in the school's softball league and used that same glove until I was 14. Teddy became an honorary uncle and my hero.

In the summer of 1935, Teddy and Eliot asked our family to have Sunday dinner with the Cohen family in Hay Lakes. Katie would provide the Jewish meal and Dave would provide the colourful stories of his life as a pedlar in Canada.

The four of us arrived at Hay Lakes, having driven on a gravel road to Cooking Lake and then on a dirt road from Cooking Lake to Hay Lakes. The road was dusty and we were cranky when we arrived around noon at the Hay Lakes Mercantile. My mother and sister were greeted by Eliot, Teddy and Hymie standing on the boardwalk by the horse trough. The women went up the store stairs to the living quarters on the second floor to meet Momma. Dad and I stayed, waiting in line by the hand-operated gasoline pumps to get Dave to fuel up our Ford model-T, a Flivver.

Dave was in his Red Strap GWG overalls, talking a blue streak and chewing on the stump of a Cuban cigar as he sold gas to the farmers. His denims were covered with oil and grease.

"Good to see you, Nelson—and your wife and kids. Teddy and Eliot have been telling me about you. We welcome you and your family. I'll fill up the Ford with gas soon," said Dave.

"Thanks for inviting us all for dinner, Dave. Teddy has been telling us about your new store."

"This place is busy; payments for goods can get a little slow but we manage with the boys helping out and doing the books. The Social Credit Party and wild Bill Aberhart are talking to the farmers around here about printing money. They have a plan; if they get into Parliament, they will make Prosperity Certificates. The other Conservative party calls it funny money. What do you think about this and the crazy Alberta politicians, Nellie?"

My dad shrugged, then drove up to the gravity-fed gas pump; Dave decided to light his cigar stump. Using a large Eddy match, he flexed his hip and lit the match on the seat of his pants. As the wooden splinter caught fire, there was a little explosion and Dave's pants caught fire.

Dad jumped out of the car as Dave's sons leaped off the boardwalk, each grabbed an arm or a leg and threw the man on fire into the horse trough. They put the fire out, even Dave's cigar stump.

Dave was at a loss for words for but a split second. Then there was a flurry of four letter words as he climbed out of the trough spluttering and complaining about the alkaline taste of Hay Lakes water. There was no more mention of So-Creds, Prosperity Certificates or the Conservatives with my father.

The financial situation was bad in Alberta in 1936. There was no money and no work. Our family decided to move for a year to New Brunswick. My mother had a job with the eastern province as a travelling drama teacher. Teddy helped drive the family in our old Ford as we headed east, but he would leave us in New York.

Unfortunately, we were in a car accident in New York. Legally, we couldn't leave the state until the litigation was over and insurance was paid to the injured party. Our family Ford was wrecked so we lived in a hotel in the city. Weeks later, after the court settlement, we took the train to Fredericton and my mother's new job. It was a sad day for me when we left New York's Central Station by train for Canada. I never saw Teddy again.

Teddy had already decided that he didn't want to practise law in Edmonton, but rather write, produce and direct plays in New York. There were no opportunities in Alberta. He wanted to be at the heart of theatre where there were many opportunities for him to be successful on Broadway and on radio. The first thing Teddy did in New York was change his name from Ted Cohen to Ted Corday. Teddy felt there was, in the city, a degree of anti-Semitism amongst radio and theatre people. With the name Corday, he probably thought he could pass himself off as a French-Canadian.

Teddy worked on Broadway for many years, mostly in radio. He successfully produced *Tortilla Flat, Tobacco Road, Gangbusters* and *Counterspy* on the airwaves.

In 1942, Teddy married Elizabeth Shay. Betty, as they called her, had been a Broadway stage actress who, as she said, "starred in one flop after another." During their 24-year marriage, Betty became a very successful producer of soap operas. Their son, Ken, was born in 1950.

After World War II, Ted teamed up with Irna Phillips. She was a teacher, business woman, actress and a talented playwright from Chicago. During the 1930's, Irna realized that in order to make a living from radio shows, she needed a sponsor and she had to maintain the copyrights to all her work. Proctor and Gamble, the multi-national soap company, decided that they needed radio advertising to sell their products—Tide, Ivory, Crest and various cosmetic products.

All the soap companies eventually branched into radio by 1951, soon, television would be the place to advertise. Irna tapped into this need for advertising by the soap companies. Her serial plays for radio were pure like the Ivory soap slogan, "99 and 44/100 percent pure," and so began the label of soap operas.

Irna's first big success was about a family, a ten-minute serial called *Painted Dreams*. In a contractual dispute with Chicago's radio station WGN, the serial was doomed when she sued over her copyrights. She lost the legal battle.

Irna was talented, however, and was the first to use "real" professionals: doctors, lawyers and ministers portrayed characters in her plays. She was very successful and very busy. She wrote about two million words a year, the equivalent of 30 novels. Starting in the late 1940's, she teamed up with Teddy Corday and Alan Chase to write the scripts. With Teddy directing, this trio produced their first great success in 1956, *As the World Turns*.

These early episodes were 30 minutes long—a psychological serial widely listened to and watched. At one time, it had an audience of ten million people per day! This serial was the second longest running soap only shadowed by *Guiding Light*, another Irna Phillips production, with well over 13,000 episodes for CBS. Proctor and Gamble still sponsored and controlled the content of the award-winning serial until its end on September 17, 2010. The conservative company resisted mention of homosexuality, abortion or divorce until well into the 1980's.

Teddy also produced three soap operas for CBS's competitor, NBC. The first two, *Paradise Bay* and *Morning Star*, flopped. The third one you may recognize, a serial called *Days of our Lives*, which was, and continues to be, a big hit. This joint effort, a melodrama, was co-created by the same trio of Irna, Alan and Teddy. This serial soap was a success right from the beginning in 1965. This became Teddy's project and was then, as it is today, produced under Corday Productions Inc. in association with Sony Pictures Television. It has received more than 40 Emmy nominations in acting, directing, writing, music and technical areas. It has won the Favourite Soap Opera Award 14 times in the 20-year history of the Emmy awards program.

Before Teddy could write many stories for his serial, he was admitted to the Cedar Sinai Medical Centre with the diagnosis of cancer. He continued to write, but he suffered a slow, lingering death and died July 23, 1966, at age 58. During this time, Betty helped him with the producing and writing of *Days of Our Lives* and co-wrote many episodes with him.

Betty continued to write and was executive producer of *Days of Our Lives* until her own death in 1987. She was also a producer for the radio soaps, *Pepper Young's Family* and *Young Doctor Malone*. In her later years, she acted as a consultant for the soap, *The Young and the Restless*. In 1985, she turned over the production and musical scores to her son, Ken.

On February 7, 2005, NBC produced the 10,000th episode of *Days of Our Lives* with executive producer and composer Ken Corday making his acting debut playing the part of a judge. Then the cast broke open the champagne and toasted the Cordays for their part in producing the longest running show on NBC–39 years of entertainment. In January of 2014, the show's contract was extended for another two years.

Ken toasted his parents, Betty and Teddy, who taught him three important lessons:

"You're only as good as your last show."
"You have to love what you are doing."
"You have to love the people you are working with."

Our family and thousands of others are proud of the two Corday brothers and their legacies.

Atlantic Number Three

Our old hunting grounds were awash in oil and mud. Duck ponds, creeks and farm stubble were splattered with petroleum and gas from Devonian subterranean reefs. In 1946 and 1947, Leduc #1 and #2 oil wells were *spudded in*, a new oil discovery in Alberta.

On March 8, 1948, Atlantic #3 blew and covered the snow and the Rebus homestead and farm, near Leduc, with muck. Atlantic #3 was a rogue well and out of control. Bulldozers of the oil industry enlarged our duck ponds. Dikes contained the black gold. Blackmud and Whitemud Creeks were contaminated with oil.

Pollution affected water purity in the North Saskatchewan River. People said it gave an added natural petroleum taste supplied by Imperial Oil and Atlantic's black lubrication. There was no place for the spring migrating ducks to land. The prairie chicken, also called the sharp-tailed grouse, the ruffed grouse, and the Hungarian partridge, had flown south—away from the immense pollution in the Edmonton area.

World War II's Holocaust was over. Were we ready for a different kind of flaming catastrophe in our own homeland? Would our big sky be screened, the sun become a murky orb, our moon be enshrouded in grit? Already our grain fields and wheat stooks were covered in tar. The smell of the air was smudgy and the taste of the water greasy. Our cherished pristine space could become an ecological crematorium.

The Leduc terrain we knew well. We were a bunch of kids who grew up on the south side of Edmonton and were students at the University of Alberta. We knew that our hunting refuge was in jeopardy. We'd been hunting there since 1942. There were five of us, all in second year at the University of Alberta. Three of the gang were gung ho engineering students, two brothers in the civil engineering program and one in mining. My best friend was taking mycology and I was a zoology major, geology minor. We were all ardent nimrods, but respectful of Alberta's bird hunting laws.

It was Labour Day, 1948, the start of the hunting season— the CBC radio's first big inaugural news story. The radio announcer declared that the outlaw Atlantic #3 of Leduc was out of control and on fire, only five months after it had blown. This was a major event and only the first day of the terrible catastrophe involving explosions and flaming oil in the Leduc fields. The whole area was ablaze. The RCMP declared the Leduc region off limits that afternoon.

I was driving an old green Pontiac when I heard the evening news on my dad's car radio: "Keep away from Atlantic #3's massive fire" was the main message. I rushed to pick up my best friends and hunting partners. These guys were always ready for anything. We didn't need maps; we knew the area, the roads and the fields. The sky was ablaze in the night, our beacon easily visible. We hit the Calgary Trail in a cloud of dust and gravel, then turned off onto dirt roads into the farm fields. We managed to avoid the cops as they combed the area for trespassers. We parked about a mile from the blaze, the car was covered in oil and dirt very quickly. Then, we piled slash and brush over the car to conceal it from the police.

We ran for a willow patch about 400-500 feet from the fire and headed down a dry creek bottom. Luckily, we were upwind from the holocaust and were able to get close. There was oil flowing everywhere. A policeman caught sight of us, but we lost him in the bulrushes growing along some ox-bow cut offs. In the effort to elude the cop, I ran into the darkness and a barbed wire fence.

I could feel blood dripping down my jeans but in the excitement of it all, I kept running. The authorities didn't challenge us again. As we got closer to the blaze, we stumbled in oil and mud until we were finally stopped by an old, coiled and barbed razor wire fence.

The sky was alight with fire. Was this a flaming volcano? Mud and oil balls shot into the night igniting lakes of surface oil. The stench of smoke and oil choked us. The heat at the core of the burning wellhead soared to 2000 degrees Fahrenheit. The wall of escaping air from the burn singed my eyebrows and my blonde moustache. I was stewing, my face aglow, my body awash in sweat. Anointed and lubricated, I was mesmerized while I cooked and the blood on my jeans caked.

In the light of this man-made volcano, all five of us stood in awe until three that morning. This flaming spectacle was etched upon my retinas and burnt in my memory. I wouldn't have missed this show...the burning of Atlantic #3.

Slowly, I drove our gang back to Edmonton, our faces blackened from the smoke and crude. We all felt that the fire and oil spill could go on forever. Our boyhood prairie hunting ground could never withstand the oil, the smoke and the heat. Sadly, we never hunted ducks, partridge or grouse there again. It took months for the fire to be snuffed out. It was only the expertise of Paul "Red" Adair and his imported Texas band of firemen that finally saved the Leduc oil fields—our cherished prairies.

63 years later, I was a passenger on a Boeing 727 landing at Edmonton International Airport in Leduc. Tarmac runways now cover the spot where the Atlantic #3 oil spill and fire occurred.

Sterling Haynes

The town of Leduc is now a city. It is a place of storage units, a pumping station for petroleum products and a dormitory for people working in Edmonton.

On the bus trip from the airport in to our Edmonton hotel, I scanned the skies and creeks looking for migrating ducks and coveys of partridge and grouse on the hunting grounds of my youth. There were no birds—that I could see. At one time, I felt like the loss of game birds in this area was permanent.

Now I know—it is forever.

'Bama Bound

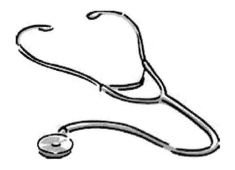

A Flattened Slug

Cadet Platoon Commander Jimmy Carter, not his real name, was a happy fellow usually. He was from "L.A."—Lower Alabama, south of the city of Selma. In a few days, he was to get his associate degree from the Marion Military Institute and a commission in the U.S. Army. As well, he would get an athletic award for his prowess as a split end on the college's winning football team.

The money he'd make in the army would help his mother and his three little brothers. No more hoeing cotton or ploughing Black Belt soil to grow sorghum and soybeans.

As the doctor for the football team, I'd admired Jimmy's happy ways and big smile. On the football field he was a fast and sure-handed receiver, but tough enough to play tight end on defense. I got to know Jimmy better late one evening at the Perry County Medical Clinic.

I asked Jimmy what the trouble was and he told me:

"About ten days ago I got a lump in the back of my neck, just below my hair line."

"Okay, take off your uniform please. Tell me how it happened."

"Doc, after my final exams my football buddies and a few regular non-coms went to Joey's bar on the edge of town. We all drank too much beer and got into a dust up with some steel workers at Cast South and then...." He paused and looked down.

"And then what happened, Jimmy?"

"Then the knives and guns came out. We were in a free for all and I got shot."

"Shot, my god, Jimmy, why didn't you come in before this? Where were you shot?"

"I took a slug in the back of my neck. It must have ricocheted off the cinder brick wall and hit me. I can feel the slug under my skin. I been trying to squeeze it out, but it's getting pretty sore."

I looked at the lump and palpated a hard mass just under the skin. It was inflamed.

"We'll get an X-ray now to see how deep it is imbedded under the skin. You'll need a tetanus booster and some ampicillin. You're not allergic to ampicillin are you?"

"No. This will be kept confidential, won't it, Doc? If any of this leaks out to General Spence or my commanding officers, my military career will be over," said the very nervous young man.

"I sympathize, Jimmy, but the sheriff has told me to report any shootings and hand over any guns and lead slugs that I find. You are asking me to break the law."

"Please, Doc, just take it out and keep it quiet. My folks depend on me. I am the first child to go to college and the first to be a commissioned officer."

"I'll consider it. First, we'll take an X-ray and locate the lead in your neck. Then I have to take the slug out."

53

"You're the doc. Usually I keep out of trouble but it's hard sometimes to be a black guy in Alabama. I'm sure you heard the KKK burned a cross on the college's golf course a month ago."

I shook my head. "Yes. Terrible."

Almost 20 years after Martin Luther King's Selma to Montgomery march, the Klan had wanted the town to know they were against the integrated college.

I opened the examining room door and beckoned Jimmy to follow. "Wanda, my nurse, will take the X-ray now." The young man walked slowly out of my office and looked around nervously.

"Don't worry, son. There's nobody here now, you're my last patient of the day. Wanda will give you a tetanus booster, too. I'll give you a prescription for ampicillin. And, please, keep your fingers off the lump. Make an appointment late on Friday and I'll take it out."

The X-ray showed a flattened slug just below the skin in the soft tissues of his neck. I put the X-ray in my bottom drawer and locked it. I had trouble sleeping over the next few days. I could lose my license if this shooting went unreported. I was in turmoil.

The following Friday Jimmy arrived for his surgery.

"Please remember to do the right thing by me, Doc."

I nodded in what I hoped was a noncommittal manner. "I'll freeze the area and take the slug out." In five minutes, I had the slug removed and the wound closed.

"So, Doc, about the sheriff..."

I thought back to Sheriff Jim Clark who ordered Martin Luther King's nonviolent marchers, women and children, beaten and tear-gassed.

"Give me a second here, Jimmy."

I thought about Jimmy Lee Jackson, a deacon from Marion, who was killed by police in February, 1965. He died because the local doctor refused to attend to him.

I unlocked my desk drawer and handed him the X-ray...and the slug. Jimmy gave me the brightest smile I had yet seen from him, and hugged me.

A few years later, I received a letter from him.

Just got promoted. Thanks for everything, Doc. Never forget what you did for me.
        Sincerely,

                Captain James Carter
                U.S. Army, Fort Bragg, North Carolina.

Sterling Haynes

An Alabama Shooting

Joe's Gro, a local convenience store, closed for the night at 11 o'clock, but the bar attached to the rural Alabama mini-market was still open two hours later. There were troubled feelings in the bar; everyone in the place could sense it. It was a broody night with clouds and intermittent rain. There was a cloying smell of stale beer and strong perfume in the heavy air. The patrons were mostly black with a sprinkling of young white military non-coms and Marine cadets from the nearby military school looking for trouble.

The military had just been paid in two-dollar bills, "the Eagle has shit," as the soldiers said, and the boys had money to burn. The cadets and non-coms believed they were invincible.

The black steel workers of Cast South Foundry knew they were just as tough. They all carried weapons. The shooting started between two African-American steel workers over a beautiful black woman.

Dark curvy velvet hips,
with bosoms silky swerves,
bloody crimson lips,
screechy rum and whisky nerves.

This is all it took
to paint the bar bright red,
sweet honeysuckle looks.
Nothing else was said.

Shotguns in the bar,
Number 8 shot in the breech,

don't need to carry far,
when you're within each other's reach.

It was over quick,
Minds done sobered fast.
Guns were all too slick,
two men's future was their past.

Sirens screamed, cops cursed the night,
Army medic crews were there and steady.
Stretchers were wheeled to the murder site,
were they dead already?

I had only recently arrived in Alabama and this was the first long weekend that I worked in Perry County Hospital's emergency room. When my first male patients arrived, they were in shock from blood loss and sucking chest wounds. The two men were blue, their breathing was noisy, and their sonorous death rasps could be heard across the room. The noise came from a massive hole in the right side of each man's chest. Blood coated the gray aluminum of the stretchers.

As these two giant African-American—the preferred term of the time was "black"—men became more cyanotic, I started the flow of oxygen at ten litres per minute by nasal catheter, then #15 intra-catheter intravenous lines in their forearms and saline infusions to keep fluid levels at some sort of normal level for the men. When Jerry, the lab tech, had completed the cross match of four units of packed cells, they were pumped rapidly into the men's arms. I ordered another eight from the blood bank at the Druid City Hospital in Tuscaloosa and four from the Selma Baptist Hospital.

I tied off their spurting blood vessels around the two massive chest holes. It was impossible to seal the holes with gauze impregnated with Vaseline, which was the usual method. Finally, I obtained Saran Wrap from the kitchen and by layering the thin plastic with Vaseline managed to get a partial seal of the sucking wounds. I then inserted a chest tube into each pleural cavity through a new incision. The tubes led to underwater seals.

I intubated both with endotracheal tubes and the nurses ventilated each man with ambu-rubber bags by hand. Despite giving each man 4000 units of packed cells and saline over four hours, they didn't improve. I replaced the plastic lung seals every 15 minutes, but by then the men's pupils became fixed and dilated—the pair were unresponsive.

I realized that there was nothing more to be done and stopped the ventilation and intravenous flows. I stood outside the emergency room in my blood-soaked scrubs, saddened by the deaths of these strong young men. I'd done all I could to save them. Never before had I treated such severe and massive gunshot wounds.

When I told all the waiting friends and relatives that the two men had died early Sunday morning, they started crying. A few strong voices broke through and the group started singing hymns. From the hospital room where I went to shower, I could hear the melody of the hymn rising above the noise of the beating water that thrummed over my tired body:

We are climbing Jacob's ladder,
We are climbing Jacob's ladder,
We are climbing Jacob's ladder,
Soldiers of the cross.

Sinner, do you love my Jesus,
Sinner, do you love my Jesus,
Sinner, do you love my Jesus,
Soldiers of the cross.

Sterling Haynes

Miss Hetty and Hushing Up

On October 15th of 1988, there was a jailbreak in Demopolis, Alabama. Two men, armed with a screwdriver, overpowered the jailer in the cellblock. Joe, the massive ringleader, tore out the old guard's larynx and left him bleeding in the jail office when the trustee tried to sound the electronic alarm. The pair took the cell keys and let themselves out.

Joe's accomplice was Robbie, a thin little guy, who had been arrested for car theft. It was Robbie who hot-wired their stolen getaway car.

They headed for Browns, Alabama and to Miss Hetty's plantation off an isolated country road. Two years before, Joe had worked for Miss Hetty as a farm labourer. He knew she was old and rich.

Hetty and her husband, Cecil, who was in a wheelchair, were alone that Saturday night. Their live-in maid had gone to a movie in Selma with the night watchman of the cotton gin, which was next door to Hetty's house. Their other three hired men lived in trailers about a mile away. Hetty and Cecil were watching the 11 o'clock news, when Joe and Robbie drove into the driveway. They kicked in the door, tore all the telephone wires out of the walls and barged into the TV room.

"Aw knows you, Miss Hetty, and we needs all your money. Aw knows you got it hid around here somewhere. You needs to give us the key to your pink Caddie, too. We won't hurt ya none, jist ya do what we say," said Joe.

"Ya, jist do what we say," echoed Robbie.

Miss Hetty was surprised, but her voice was steady and as precise as her blue-rinsed white bouffant hairdo.

"You just leave Cecil be, he's had a stroke and he wouldn't hurt a fly. We just saw your picture on the TV just now. The sheriff's posse and the state troopers are looking for y'all."

"Don't mess with us, Miss Hetty. We needs the car keys and your cash now," said Joe.

"Ya, don't mess with us," said Robbie, with a quaver in his voice.

"I have a little ready cash that I keep in a special secret compartment in the back of that desk drawer over there. I carry the keys in my purse for the desk and my Cadillac. You can watch me get the money from the secret compartment. If you let me open my purse in front of you, I'll give you my car keys and the key to the garage."

"Yas, okay, Miss Hetty. Don't try no funny business or I'll break your husband's arm, y'all hear."

"What could an old lady and a crippled husband do to the likes of you two? Here are the car keys. Just let me go over to my desk nice and slowly and get you the money, okay?"

"Shore nuff, Miss Hetty, take it slow, no funny business now."

Miss Hetty walked over to her massive oak desk and unlocked the top drawer. "It'll take me a few minutes to locate the special secret compartment. Y'all understand."

"Shore do," said Robbie.

"Be quick about it, I hear dogs a'brayin' and a'barkin'," said Joe.

"It's just our hounds George and Jeb carrying on, I won't be just a minute. You boys got nothing to worry about." Miss Hetty reached deep into the top drawer. There was an audible click.

"What was that, Miss Hetty?"

"Oh, nothing...just me releasing the desk catch and getting into my secret place."

Miss Hetty turned, brandishing her Saturday night special, and steadying the gun with her left hand, she shot Joe between the eyes. She then turned the gun on Robbie and winged him in the shoulder before he dove through the window.

Joe was dead. His red blood had started to stain her Persian rug. She quickly crumpled up the Marion town newspaper and stuffed it under Joe's head. *The rug will have to be cleaned*, she thought, as she reloaded her .38-caliber revolver.

The three spent cartridge cases dropped beside the corpse. The sound of the dogs grew louder and now she could hear the sirens blaring. She fingered her bouffant. *Yes, not a hair out of place.*

Hetty used a linen hankie to wipe the moisture from her upper lip. Her mascara had started to run from her tears as she dabbed her cheeks with the hanky. Finally, she was ready to meet that new state trooper and give her statement to him.

I confirmed that Joe was DOA at the Perry County Hospital. Robbie was only slightly wounded. As the ER doctor that night, I notified the state coroner. Over the next few weeks, I didn't hear anything about an autopsy, an inquest or an ongoing police investigation.

Details of violence can get "hushed up some" in the Black Belt of rural Alabama—especially if there is violence and a white woman involved. At least that is what the state trooper told me.

I watched the Marion weekly newspaper for the next month, but there was no notice or article describing the jailbreak— or the shooting death of the massive convict named Joe.

It was "hushing up time" in Dixieland.

Miss Lillian

I was surprised to find that the U.S. Army and the Federal Health Development Corporation had built a modern clinic with three offices for me and the staff. It was equipped with a modern lab and a state-of-the-art General Electric X-ray unit. My duties were to look after the people of Perry County and the cadets of Marion Military Institute (MMI). This high school and junior college was nicknamed "My Mother Insisted." I was elated. This was much more luxurious than the cramped quarters I had shared with 24 other doctors in Kamloops.

I should have suspected that something was different when I found the waiting room held over 60 comfortable chairs. We had air conditioning, flush toilets, ice water fountains and the first desegregated waiting room in the county. The county was poor— many African-Americans, Blacks or Negroes—the vernacular of the time, lacked phones to make appointments. So when they were sick, they just came to the clinic and waited in the coolness and enjoyed the icy water and indoor plumbing.

The people were stoic; some came and waited all day if they had to. Sometimes I was only able to see the very sickest people and had to tell the rest that they would have to come back the next morning. My wife and I closed the office for the night at eight or nine o'clock each evening.

Some of my paying patients were loyal, but many of the people with good insurance health policies were inclined to be difficult...and Caucasian. I seldom found my African-American patients to be anything but polite.

I was introduced to Miss Lillian by her sister Ruth, who had been one of my first patients. Ruth learned to trust me when I diagnosed her iron deficiency anaemia and her recurrent deep thrombophlebitis of her leg as secondary to cancer of the transverse colon. Ruth was referred to a Baptist Montgomery surgeon for a successful operation and chemotherapy. She was the intellectual of her family and headed the Social Security section of the federal government offices in Selma. Miss Ruth and I were friends.

Her younger sister, Miss Lillian, was different from Ruth, I might say this aged white debutante was *ruthless*.

Miss Lillian was coquettish and still interested in men, although she had reached the respectable age of 70. She was a bridge player, gin drinker and social leader for the Methodist church in the town of Marion. Miss Lillian was always made up; her silver-rinsed hair was piled high on her head; diamond rings adorned most of her fingers. On her ring finger, she had a bright two-carat diamond that outshone the other diamonds, but the same finger had no gold band on display. They say that her martini glass was always in her left hand at parties to display this magnificent stone surrounded, like stars, with smaller, glittering finger-twinklers on both hands.

I once asked Miss Lillian how many times she had been engaged. I immediately realized that I had made a grave mistake when I saw the scowl on her face—she never answered my abrasive question.

Miss Lillian and her sister lived in a magnificent antebellum home on Main Street across from their church. She often talked of her family's plantation on the outskirts of the town's Black Belt that produced tons of sorghum, soybean and corn. Three crops a year kept her family coffers full. She talked of the gentry and the local people who were as wealthy as she was. I am sure she considered me a foreigner, a skilled plebeian sent to her universe to care for her ills. In Alabama, there is a saying among the moneyed class: "You're born rich, live poor and die rich." This was not the case with Miss Lillian—she loved to flaunt her wealth and position.

In my medical office, there was sometimes conflict between Miss Lillian and my nurse of colour, Wanda.

"Please don't refer to Wanda as my girl," I told Miss Lillian. "Please call her Nurse or perhaps Wanda. She is a valuable member of our health care team."

"Yes, Doctor, but you mustn't forget you are in Dixieland now. The white people of Marion have always been like this. We are jammed up here and jelly tight in your clinic. I wish you had a bit more separation between the groups here in your office like my previous doctor, God rest his soul."

"Do you mean segregation? Do you mean you want me to have separate restrooms and water fountains? Would you prefer that the black people must come to the clinic after five o'clock and that they should enter by the alley door? Is that what you mean, Miss Lillian?"

"You make it sound so bad, Doctor. But last week, I had to see a young black girl in your waiting room with an earthworm coming out her nose. The vision upset me so much that it destroyed my bridge game later that afternoon. My bridge partner and I lost the rubber match on account of that little black girl and I couldn't finish my martini."

"That little girl had an infestation of intestinal round worms called *Ascaris*. She needed medical treatment. We will not allow segregation in this clinic, Miss Lillian. I can send your records elsewhere any time you wish."

"Doctor, please don't upset yourself. I was just asking. My sister Ruth likes you and your girl said you are available close by for house calls when I really get sick. You know, we live in that large house on Main Street. I'm sure you know it, Doctor, the white mansion, across from the largest church in town."

"Usually, I make house calls where the people have no means of transportation and they are old and frail. Your driver and your pink Cadillac will find ample room for parking at our clinic if you have need to see me. Now what is your medical problem today, Miss Lillian?"

Sterling Haynes

Voodoo Medicine

In 1980, when we moved to rural Alabama, I didn't know my competition was to be Dr. Buzzard and Voodoo medicine.

Dr. Buzzard was a prominent healer, a conjure man, from the Sea Islands in South Carolina. His medicine could be purchased in small rural stores in Dixieland at a typical "Joe's Gro." Medical advice, hexes, chants, dolls with long hat pins could be purchased from Dr. Buzzard by phone or by mail for ten dollars prepaid—cash only. His medicine claimed to turn bad hexes into good hexes, bad blood into good and it could "get fat off, too." Dr. Buzzard's snake oil remedies and *juju* items were popular and dispensed through his mail order catalogue, as well.

Moonshine, another "drug," was made locally on Buckaloo Mountain and the hills of Alabama. It was also readily available for one dollar in the parking lots, after hours, at the Piggly Wiggly supermarkets, as well as a few isolated, independent grocery stores.

Soon I got to know about cock fights and dog fights held at clandestine rural locations from conversations with my patients and my nurse, Wanda. Usually *juju* remedies, hexes and moonshine were readily available at intermissions between bouts and after the fights, Wanda told me one day.

Seldom did the local police intervene in this illegal sport, though Alabama state troopers would occasionally show up and serve out tickets and make arrests. Moonshine was the drink of choice during matches and could be used to wash down Dr. Buzzard's foul-tasting medicines.

One morning I arrived at my Perry Medical Clinic office to look for a medical chart—it was six o'clock. Earlier, at midnight, a patient had died unexpectedly in the emergency room of the hospital. The family was very upset with me about the sudden death of their 80-year-old daddy. His sons claimed I hadn't done enough to save him.

On the sidewalk outside my office door this fine morning lay a headless chicken—it had been eviscerated. I could see blood sprayed on the exterior of the clinic's cement walls and windows. This was a Dixieland hex. Maybe this was just a *juju* warning, as nothing evil seemed to befall our family, or me, upon occasions like these. Nurse Wanda did not seem overly concerned about the chicken blood and put it down to "those crazy, country folks."

I knew that Dr. Buzzard produced and sold bottles of "Jinx Killers" as well as "John the Conqueror Spiritual Incense" locally, but I never had a patient with an overdose from the concoctions. The medicine made on the Sea Islands of South Carolina, the snake oil medicine, must have been harmless even though patients said "it tasted real bad."

I soon learned the opposite was true of the moonshine made in the mountains. It was truly dangerous. The stills were old. For making this liquor, the bootleggers used old lead pipes in the fermenting and bottling of the product. The liquor was so potent and toxic that it also ate the lead from the old pipes in the still.

After a series of rural late night cock fights, I had a number of drinking men appear at the clinic over a few days with complaints of severe tingling in their extremities. They were also suffering severe cramps: They called the colic "wandering farts." Wanda told me that these men, drank a lot of moonshine and lead poisoning was common in Perry County.

Markedly elevated blood lead levels confirmed my diagnosis of peripheral neuritis and of colic due to lead poisoning. I started treatment by first warning the men that their booze source was poisonous due to the lead content. Then I started treatment with a chelating agent called BAL (British-Anti-Lewisite or dimercapol), which removed the lead from the victim. All the men recovered. I notified the public health officer for Perry County. Soon, Alabama state troopers were searching for and destroying illicit stills in the isolated hills.

Dr. Buzzard continued to supply medicine to the folk in the south and became a multimillionaire Voodoo doctor. His medicine seemed to be harmless compared to the local hooch.

Finally, his supplies of medicine slowly dried up when the police in South Carolina stopped the sale of his snake oil in the Carolinas, Georgia, Alabama and Mississippi. The authorities brought him to trial in South Carolina, but nobody would testify in court. The local people were afraid of reprisals. The charges of income tax evasion were also dropped. Nobody would claim they bought any of his products for fear of hexes and evil torments being put on them by Dr. Buzzard.

The sheriff's office on the Sea Islands finally got a conviction against conjure doctors with the help of the state of South Carolina's Medical Association. Dr. Buzzard and his colleague, Dr. Snake, went to jail for "practising medicine without a licence."

Martin and Alabama Medicine

Because we have tasted the bitter swill of civil war and segregation, and emerged from that dark chapter stronger and more united, we cannot help but believe that the old hatreds shall someday pass; and the lines of the tribe shall soon dissolve; that, as the world grows smaller. Our common humanity shall reveal itself...

—Barack Obama, Presidential Inaugural Address, 2009

At our clinic, the first desegregated one in town, as I mentioned in an earlier story, we were swamped from day one and the waiting room chairs were mostly filled. Anyone could sit in our waiting room and on our toilet seats, too!

The Alabama lingo we heard was hard "to cotton on to." "Y'all doing all right?" and "What do you know good?" were the usual greetings. The negative answer to my questions took a little time to figure out. "Sure don't" was more common than "Sure do."

One of the first couples to see me in the clinic was Obadiah and Bernice Scott. They had serious medical problems and were octogenarians. They asked me to discuss all their medical problems with their daughter, Coretta Scott King, the widow of the late Reverend Martin Luther King Jr. Coretta and I spoke every few weeks over the phone. Over the years, I got to know the life of the Scotts and the Kings and the history of "the day the lights went out in Marion."

Obie and Bernice Scott lived just out of town and ran a "Joe's Gro"—a kind of Alabama 7-11. Obie told me that he'd never been robbed because he packed a Magnum .44 and practiced shooting targets when business was slow. On their first visit, we established that I was from British Columbia, Canada (not Colombia, South America, a common misconception in the town). As we chatted, Obadiah told me he thought I was all right and maybe he and Bernice would change doctors and become my patients. He ended by saying, "Just call me Obie, Doc."

While treating Obie and Bernice, I became interested in the Freedom March.

"The Night the Lights Went Out in Marion," was the headline used in newspapers across the globe on February 18, 1965. Over 300 nonviolent people had gathered in Marion's town square to protest the laws of Perry County which prevented 98 percent of the African-American community from voting in any election. Large spotlights shone on the Marion courthouse and gave light to the demonstration in the square. The people were linked together singing "We Shall Overcome," and Dr. King's favourite gospel song, "Follow the Drinking Gourd." During the singing, Alabama state troopers shot out the many large spotlights and unleashed their nightsticks from waist holsters.

In the melee that followed, 26-year-old Jimmie Lee Jackson, a church deacon, was arrested for trying to protect his mother from being beaten by the troopers and their wielded nightsticks. He was taken to the local jail, arrested, and then shot twice in the belly by trooper James Fowler. Both bullet burns on Jackson's belly skin indicated, later, he was shot from no more than four feet away. The two wounds of exit on his back were reported to be monstrously large.

Jackson was taken to the Marion Hospital, but the doctor on call refused to attend to his wounds. He was transferred to the Good Samaritan Hospital, 18 miles away, in Selma. He died there eight days later, at the "Good Sam." No attempt was made to surgically close the large holes in Jackson's belly. Trooper Fowler was tried, but not convicted. In 2009, Fowler was retried, convicted of murder and received a jail sentence of nine months.

In response to the death of Jimmie Lee Jackson, activists led by Hosea Williams and John Lewis led a march from Selma to the state capital of Montgomery, a distance of 55 miles. In Selma, they were stopped by Sheriff Jim Clark and his deputies, aided by state troopers led by Major John Cloud. Reportedly, the manner in which the march was halted was brutal—incognito Ku Klux Klan members lined the streets to watch policemen beat the marchers with cane whips and night sticks. Troopers on horseback flailed backs. This "Freedom March" was stopped at the Pettus Bridge crossing the Alabama River.

This police brutality, including use of tear gas, was sanctioned by then Alabama Governor, George Wallace.

That evening thugs beat Boston protester James Reeb with baseball bats and lead pipes. Reverend Reeb, a Unitarian minister, died in a Selma hospital two days later from his head injuries.

On March 21, the protesters assembled at the Red Church in downtown Selma for the walk to Montgomery—this march was sanctioned by President Lyndon B. Johnson. The 25,000 demonstrators were protected by hundreds of FBI agents and the federalized Alabama National Guardsmen. They travelled up to 17 miles a day and at night were entertained by the presence and songs of Lena Horne and Harry Belafonte.

The final rally was held at the steps of the Capital building at Montgomery where Reverend Martin Luther King declared: "The end we seek is a society at peace with itself that can live with its conscience. And that will not be the day of the white man nor the day of the black man. That will be the day of man as man."

On August 6, President Lyndon B. Johnston, recalling the outrage at Selma, signed the Voting Rights Act of 1965. All members of every race in America's south would now be allowed to vote without harassment by politicians, the Klan or police.

Reverend King continued his plea for equality and was successful in Dixieland until April 4, 1968. On that spring day, the magnolias were blooming, and the sanitation workers were striking in Memphis for decent pay and working conditions. Reverend King was preparing his speech to the sanitation workers in the Lorraine Motel.

As he stepped out onto the balcony of the motel, he was shot in the neck with a single 30.30 bullet. The rifle shot came from a flophouse across the street. King died instantly. Within hours, riots occurred in cities across the U.S. in protest of their spiritual leader's death. Perhaps King had predicted his death when months before he said, "I've been to the top of the mountain and I've looked over and I've seen the Promised Land. I may not make it there with you, but you will get to the Promised Land."

James Earl Ray, drifter with a prison record, was convicted of murder. Ray had been stalking King for months.

Obie and Bernice were very proud of Coretta and Martin. When I think of the Scotts, I think of Martin's great speech given before 2000,000 people in 1963 at the Lincoln Memorial Center in Washington, DC. King's speech exemplified the philosophy of the

Scotts: "I have a dream that one day this nation will rise up and live out the true meaning of its creed. We hold that these truths be self-evident, that all men are created equal...."

When we left Alabama in 1990, Bernice brought a pound cake and hugs. Obie brought us a watermelon and gave me a firm handshake. As he left the clinic, he turned and said he had something to tell me.

"What is it, Obie?" I asked, concerned.

"You're the first whitey I ever trusted."

Many years later, his statement still echoes in my assisted hearing ears...etched upon my soul: I consider it an honour that this 92-year-old man trusted me when other white men had vilified and beaten his son-in-law. The KKK, with their head office in nearby Tuscaloosa, regularly terrorized black activists and a white man had shot and killed Martin Luther King Jr. I am not sure if I would have been so magnanimous had I been wearing Obadiah Scott's shoes.

Weapons of Destruction

A 'Nam veteran man appears in my Alabama medical office wearing old frayed battle dress with the chevrons of a corporal sewn on the sleeves. He is smoking a joint and the sweet smell of pot smoke invades the office.

"What can I do for you today, Corporal?" I ask him.

"What da ya know good, Doc? My dogs won't hunt and Mary and the kids won't talk to me. Me, I'm just aging out, hanging around the bars. I'm no account, Doc. Mary...she done got a new man friend, she thinks I don't know. She does still excite me–but I can't do nothin', Doc.

"And those goddamned headaches have started again. Every night I have nightmares, the headaches start and carry over 'til morning. It's always the same thing, Doc–the killin', the hollerin', the wounded, the noise and the blowing sand. Them two-bit plastic mines—I hate 'em, hate 'em. They's diabolical, they blew my foot off and went up into my privates. They took my balls and dink off, excuse the language, Doc. I'm no good for nothing. President Johnson shipped me home with a pension from the United States Army. The Marines and the Veterans Affairs don't have no answers. The hospital in Pasagoula ain't got room for me. I'm a Mississippi psycho, Doc! Let's face it. Ah got no place to go.

"I can't get the war out of my head...flashbacks of feet, arms, balls lying among the dead. Vultures in the sky land to feed on the bodies. Them damned birds fighting among themselves for the eyes of the dead in the bloody sand. Even now the memory of guts makes me want to puke. Them winds can't blow nothin' away offa my mind. I gotta do somethin', my nerves is shot.

"You'd snort coke if you was me, Doc. No balls and peeing through a hole between my legs. I get urges but it's all in my head. Just limp aroun' the town 'til the bars open, then drink and play pool. Maybe go to a crack house if my pension check comes in. Ya don't mind if I light up a joint? Had to get that off my chest, Doc. And Doc, all this bullshit army propaganda on the TV, it don't mean nothin'."

The corporal stops talking. He flicks the joint onto the lino floor and grinds it under his boot. He begins to cry and then sob uncontrollably. Just as I start to tell him what I can do to help, he stands up and leaves.

I follow him out of the office and try to reason with him but he leaves quickly. I hear the roar of a Harley-Davidson motorcycle as he starts it up and guns the machine down the hill.

Sterling Haynes

The Free VD Clinic
or
My Life as a Dick Doc

The fires of Venus were burning brightly when I arrived in Marion. In 1981, the U.S. Army brass enlisted me to put out the diseased flames at the proposed site of a new VD clinic. With army input and the expertise of the Health Development Corporation, I was sure we could douse the flames.

The clinic, on Magnolia Street, I soon discovered, had been closed for years and the building that housed the office was derelict. It was far from new. The sign advertising the clinic was hanging sideways, held by a giant clip attached to a rusty piece of iron sticking out from the building. The sign blew in the wind, making a clanking sound. The attending doctor's name was listed on a bronze plaque on the front door. He had been dead for years.

The public health officer and the U.S. Army health officer asked me to please open the clinic for at least two hours a week. I agreed, but stipulated that I would only be able to see ten patients in two hours. The officers wanted to change the name to "The Sexually Transmitted Infectious Disease Clinic." The newly-repaired sign couldn't accommodate all these words so the powers-that-be restored the old words.

The new sign read: "The VD Clinic (free)." The cracked and broken windows were replaced, new mortar patched the bricks, the trim and the floors were painted. Much of the old graffiti showed through the single coat of paint on the walls. New opaque plastic curtains were put up and we received cases of paper gowns, disposable sheets and 2,000 plastic, extra-large, disposable vaginal speculi—one size fits all. Another box contained 10,000 un-sized condoms. Artificial purple tulips were installed in all the offices and examining rooms to give ambiance to the place.

To treat my patients, I had to learn idioms of the Deep South. "High blood" meant elevated blood pressure, while "low blood" equalled anaemia, in young patients perhaps sickle cell anaemia. "Bad blood" was syphilis. "Fireballs" meant uterine fibroids.

"Don't mash my fireballs," meant I was not to do a pelvic examination with deep palpation. When a man complained of a "dripping faucet," he likely had gonorrhoea. "Roaches of the liver," meant cirrhosis of the liver and "gouch" was gout. I soon learned the vernacular and how to swim through the muddy waters of *Alabamese*, but with difficulty.

We did a lot of testing in the clinic: taking cultures for gonorrhoea, dark field microscopy for syphilitic sores and wet preps for vaginal discharges. I tested my patients for syphilis, HIV/AIDS and did a simple urine test for pregnancy. I took Pap smears to screen for cervical cancer. When we first opened, I was astounded at the number of tests that were positive.

One morning, I was surprised when ten young men appeared looking for a "dick Doc" and the one ex-Navy veteran looking for a "chancre mechanic."

Their knowledge of what they had was right on. All ten had primary syphilitic sores on their penises. We took smears for *Treponema pallidum* and dark field microscopy and drew blood to test for syphilis. When spirochaetes were found on microscopy, I started treatment, giving each man shots of three million units of procaine penicillin over ten days. I also prescribed probenecid. I notified the public health officer in Selma and asked him to follow up with all the patients and their contacts.

The following week, a young woman appeared at the clinic.

"Doc, ah heard you is an expert on VD and dicks. The health nurse in Selma sent me here cause I got sores on my privates and my mouth, my monkey itches and I got a blue waffle. Can you help, Doc?"

"I can certainly help with the sores on your lips. But what is a blue waffle?"

"A blue waffle means everything got curdled in my big 'O' and ah cain't stop scratching."

"Well, we'll have to take tests from your vaginal discharge and some blood tests. I'll need to examine you as well."

"Don't mash too hard now. Doc, please."

Her tests showed her vaginal emulsion contained gonorrhoea, moniliasis and trichonads. Her sores tested positive for *T. pallidum.* She was a triple threat vaginally and she had very contagious syphilis to add to the trio of maladies. I began treatment for all the diseases and asked her to stop all intercourse. I also asked her to inform the public health nurse in Selma about her male contacts.

In 1983, we started doing HIV testing and seeing AIDS patients. The three men that I looked after were dying of AIDS despite early anti-viral treatment. The medication was supplied free of charge by the state of Alabama's infectious disease specialist in Montgomery. I probably phoned him twice a week for advice. The early treatment he recommended did not slow down the disease and the men wasted away. Over the few months I saw them, the men lost 50-60 pounds and were plagued by *Herpes zoster*. Shingles was virulent in these men and treatment consisted of doses of morphine for the continual nerve pain they suffered.

One man soon developed Kaposi's sarcoma and the purplish lesions appeared on his feet, legs and in his mouth, accompanied by numerous enlarged lymph nodes. His family looked after him at home. They wanted no further treatment for him and I gave the family members a prescription for morphine injections to ease the pain in his final days. He was comfortable until the end.

The second patient left the area to be with his mother and father, who farmed in Perry County. He died very quickly.

The third man, a Caucasian, came to Marion to be looked after by his elderly mother. They lived for a short time in his mother's trailer. The rednecks in the trailer park harassed them continually. Finally, late at night, a group of men insisted that Jeremy leave the trailer park. At this time, he had Kaposi's sarcoma, untreatable shingles and suffered constant pain.

The next day Jeremy appeared in my office to tell me about the confrontation.

Sterling Haynes

"Doc, I thought those men were going to lynch me. Things got ugly, Doc. Mom tried to talk them down but it was of no use. They threatened to burn our place down."

I had phoned the owner of the trailer park and explained that AIDS was not contagious unless people were exposed to the virus in bodily secretions. The owner seemed to understand, but from the gossip and rumours I heard about town, many people didn't. I heard tell that the Klan was getting involved and, indeed, a few days later burned a cross in town. Jeremy's sister took him to her house where she and her mother looked after him.

When Jeremy developed a fungus type of pneumonia (a pneumocystitis infection), the family elected to treat him with oxygen and morphine. Sadly, Jeremy developed dementia and later died of his pneumonia. He weighed only 70 pounds. Although he was raised in Marion, his funeral was sparsely attended.

Our health care team continued to offer free services at the clinic. We were taxed and had to limit the patient number to 20 on any given day. Most Thursdays I missed lunch but after these gruelling sessions...I had little appetite. When I retired nine years later, the clinic closed. None of the local doctors wanted to run The VD Clinic (free).

"Willie's Puddle" & Persons, Places & Things That Moved Me

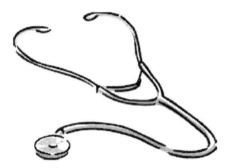

Hank

I first met Heinrich "Hank" Mueller in the ramshackle War Memorial Hospital in Williams Lake in April of 1961. Hank was a huge logger who had come to Canada to make his fortune. He had left the gymnasiums of Germany and immigrated to the new world to become a lumber baron at the age of 20.

The first thing Hank did, after he set up his two-man sawmill around a stand of white Horsefly cedar, was to remove the safety guards around the head saw. Hank and his buddy had cut the huge cedar logs over the winter and piled them in his booming yard beside a small pond. Hank and his partner, Jake, were ready to "highball" in their new mill. After a month of cutting cedar, the mill site was a mess of slabs, branches and sawdust. The piles of sawn lumber were huge. In their eagerness to make money, they had neglected cleanup and repairs. The raised ramp that the men stood on to feed the logs into the head saw had a broken plank.

Through the hole in the ramp, the oily moving chain was visible. This chain connected the diesel motor to the sprocket of the giant head saw. The log carriage with the two containing "dogs" controlled the huge cedar logs as they were fed into the giant head saw to make cedar cants, usually 12-by-12 inch square beams.

One day, the "dogs" on the carriage jammed when a giant cedar log got stuck. Instead of shutting down the saw, Hank attempted to turn the log with a *pea-vie* by brute strength. The rickety ramp was covered with water and oil. The *pea-vie* was ripped out of his hands and his left leg fell through the wet broken ramp. The ragged cuff of his denim pants hooked onto the chain, which dragged Hank's leg into the rapidly revolving sprocket, turning the head saw. By the time Jake had shut off the diesel and the saw, Hank's leg had been amputated at the hip. The leg had been chewed up and spit out into the sawdust pile along with a portion of Hank's scrotum.

Hank screamed as Jake took off his wool shirt and wound it around the bleeding stump, twisting it as a tourniquet over the spurting femoral artery. When the bleeding had stopped, a panicked Jake carried his partner to the pickup truck and drove him the 30 miles to the hospital.

Arriving at the hospital entrance, Jake half carried this giant man into the corridor. Hank managed to hop on one leg to the stretcher until he collapsed on the hard mattress of the gurney with his bleeding stump prominent.

I was fresh from a California residency in medicine and paediatrics. I had seldom seen such a horrible mangling of the human body. I started intravenous saline with a large bore needle and quickly ordered four units of blood and a complete blood count. The femoral artery was oozing through the flannel shirt tourniquet. I removed Hank's shirt and caught the spurting artery with a Kelly clamp. I had the lab tech cross match and then gave him four units of blood. Dr. Barney Ringwood, a local surgeon, arrived to trim the stump and repair Hank's empty scrotum. We then transferred him to the care of orthopaedic surgeon Hammy Boucher at the Vancouver General Hospital.

When Hank left the Cariboo Memorial Hospital, he thanked all the staff and told us: "When I come back with my new leg, I'm going to build a hunting and fishing lodge. Me and Jake are going to get our big game guiding licenses. All you people are welcome to come out to fish and be my guest."

When Hank returned, he had adapted to his prosthesis and went back to work as a big game guide, trapper and sometime logger in the Horsefly area.

About two years later, he and Jake were guiding four Portland policemen on a moose and deer hunt around Horsefly Lake. At dusk, disaster struck again. One of the policemen had gone out to find yet another moose to take back home and mistakenly shot two pack horses...and Jake. Hank put the bleeding Jake in his truck and drove him to the hospital. When they arrived, Jake was close to death. We tried cardiac resuscitation and five blood transfusions, but he died a few hours later.

The American policemen went back to Portland with two tons of moose burgers. No charges were laid, as far as I know. It was labelled a "bad accident" by the local newspaper. The ex-cop coroner called it a case of "accidental misadventure."

Frontier Anaesthesia (Passing Gas)

Passing gas can be hard to do at any time, but for the part-time general practitioner anaesthetist in rural Canada, sometimes, it can be a big pain! Even more difficult to master is the anaesthetic's recovery phase, as The Larynospasms, a doctor and nurse quintet, sing "Waking Up is Hard to Do."

When giving a general anaesthetic with paralyzing drugs, there can be many complications, especially in the very young or elderly. The anaesthetist can have variable problems—seconds of absolute terror when the patient turns blue, for example, interspersed with hours of absolute boredom. Generally, regional, spinal, epidural and local anaesthetics are relatively easy to administer. Putting people to sleep with a general anaesthetic can be difficult, but waking them up is even harder.

When I first arrived at Williams Lake in 1960, the only experience I had in giving anaesthetics was as an intern in Edmonton's Royal Alexandra Hospital. I'd had a superb teacher, Dr. Cal Fletcher, one of the hospital staff anaesthetists. I administered many ether generals and intubated hundreds of kids and adults. Nothing had prepared me later for the anaesthetics I had to give at the Williams Lake War Memorial Hospital.

In Williams Lake, I usually gave open drop ether by a Schimmelbusch gauze mask after the sodium pentothal intravenous induction. To get the patient *into the deep*, the fourth and final, stage of ether anaesthesia could be difficult. Some doctors dripped alcohol and chloroform on the masks. This combination was called "one, two, three" (ether, alcohol and chloroform) and was extremely potent. Chloroform caused all kinds of heart arrhythmias and I refused to use it, even on the big, strong loggers that came to the hospital. We had no endotracheal tubes, no Boyle-manufactured anaesthetic machines or any respirators.

Early in my career in Williams Lake, I gave an anaesthetic to a logger with a broken leg. To ascertain the depth of ether anaesthesia, I tested the corneal reflex in his eye. Using a wisp of cotton wool held between my thumb and forefinger, I stroked his cornea. Later in the recovery room, the patient told me that he had a great anaesthetic except for the fact that as he was drifting off to sleep "some stupid S.O.B. stuck his finger in my eye." I never tested the corneal reflex that way again.

I decided some further training was needed, so in 1961, I went to the Vancouver General Hospital to learn from UBC's Dr. Horkey Graves. A few months later, I studied with certified anaesthetists Drs. Allen Thomas and Norman Thorntons at the Royal Inland Hospital in Kamloops. These three docs made me into a safe anaesthetist. I used anectine and curare, which paralyzed the patients. Then I intubated them and introduced cyclopropane, an inhalation agent, or ether, and I breathed for them. I insisted that the hospital purchase a Boyle anaesthetic machine and a graded set of sized endotracheal tubes. Years later, the hospital brought in halothane. With this new inhalation product, passing gas became much easier.

Cyclopropane was relatively mild and safe, except for the fact that it is also highly explosive. My first effort using "cyclo" was terrifying. The dilapidated Williams Lake Hospital had no grounded electrical outlets or special electrical grounding in the floor.

By chance, one of the young OR nurses had just bought a tight-fitting silk uniform which she wore under the usual green cotton OR gown. I had given the patient pentothal and anectine in preparation for passing the endotracheal tube and I was bagging him with pure oxygen when it happened. I had just switched over to cyclopropane when this nurse touched me on the shoulder. A large spark flew from her silk dress to me to the oxygen and cyclo. There was a huge explosion of cyclopropane and oxygen. My left hand holding the mask on the patient was blown upward and the rubber resuscitation bag blew off the Boyle anaesthetic machine. The young patient suffered no ill effects and was discharged the next day with no respiratory problems. I was shaken by the event. Fifty years later, I still have nightmares. I rarely used cyclo again.

Over the years in the OR I learned not to swear, even when confronted with emergencies. Fifty years ago I gave a spinal anaesthetic to a young woman, Trish, with a tubal ectopic pregnancy. She had gone into shock from blood loss and I told the nurses to run to the lab and get the "goddamned blood."

When the patient woke up, she reminded me that I had used bad language. Trish recanted her experiences as a "near death experience" when she phoned me after my first book came out half a century later.

On another occasion, I was giving an ether anaesthetic to a 13-year-old First Nations boy for a tonsillectomy. He was a fit young lad who had suffered bouts of quinsy through the winter months. I gave my patient, Billy, an induction of sodium pentothal, then a small dose of anectine, also called succinylcholine, to paralyze him. I put him on oxygen, intubated him and switched to ether.

The surgeon took the tonsils out by dissection and snare, the bleeding was minimal and the procedure took about 20 minutes. When the anaesthetic seemed to lighten, I extubated him, but to no avail. Billy refused to start breathing spontaneously. I conferred with my partner, Hugh Atwood. We were both in a quandary. I had to re-intubate Billy a number of times as he refused to breathe on his own.

We kept bagging him for seven or eight hours until I finally phoned my mentor, Dr. Horkey Graves, for help.

"Sterling, I think your Billy represents a rare case of a deficiency of plasma cholinesterase. The anectine is not being metabolized by cholinesterase. Please give him plasma cholinesterase contained in the form of a litre of blood and he should soon be able to breathe on his own."

I thanked him and made immediate arrangements to cross match his blood. I gave Billy a blood transfusion. He soon woke up and when he began to breathe on his own, I gave out a huge sigh of relief.

Yes, waking up can be very hard...very hard to do.

The Chapel and the Morgue

The War Memorial Hospital in Williams Lake once had a small clapboard building on its grounds. It was painted gray at one point in time, but over the years the paint had peeled and faded.

The building was connected to the hospital by a 100-foot wooden sidewalk with missing slats: These holes could catch a foot or ankle and trip unsuspecting morticians, doctors and religious leaders. The small building housed the chapel on one side and the morgue on the other. It lacked heat and water, and dim lighting was provided by four 40-watt bulbs. It could be difficult to find your way in the chapel on dark nights and a wrong turn could take you to the morgue. Those dead bodies could be disconcerting for those who came to pray for the sick...not at, or to, the dead.

According to my partner, Dr. Hugh Atwood, the morgue and chapel were built by Countess Beatrice Calonna di Montecchio—a wealthy English woman formerly married to an Italian nobleman. The countess ran an isolated tourist lodge at Timothy Lake in the Cariboo, just east of the San Jose River and Lac La Hache. Her American partner and lover helped in the running of the lodge. His name was Lloyd "Cyclone" Smith, and he was from the state of Washington.

Cyclone was quite a character. He was a wrangler, bronco buster and rodeo rider, and manager of the Williams Lake Stampede Grounds. On June 29, 1932, Cyclone was riding as a pickup man, attempting to corral a riderless bucking bronco during a Stampede event. The horses collided, Cyclone fell and his skull was crushed as the horses went down on top of him. Cyclone's 37-year-old body was laid out on a cold cement slab in the local blacksmith's shop to the dismay of the countess.

In memory of her lover, and her earlier departed brother, she had a small morgue and chapel built by the hospital. On the half wall separating the morgue from the chapel was the white dress uniform, with sword and scabbard, of her deceased drowned brother, Lieutenant E.C. Evans, Royal Naval Reserve. Beside this was a brass plaque with the inscription, "My Best Pal." On the opposite full wall in the chapel was a photo of Cyclone Smith, in cowboy regalia, carrying a saddle in one hand and a ten-gallon hat in the other. His bridle, stirrups and saddle were also hung on the wall and his brass plaque read: "A courageous, honest man, a good scout and ideal companion."

When asked to do an autopsy, I was faced with cold, poor lighting and no running water. The chapel was cleaner and better lit than the morgue. There were three rows of oak pews on either side of a central aisle. A large clean white-clothed table was centremost at the front of the chapel. The entrance to the morgue was covered by an old canvas curtain stained with blood and covered with grease-stained fingerprints. The tin metal autopsy table in the morgue was crudely made and on it was a two-by-four piece of lumber, the body's head rest. There were a couple of metallic water buckets to help with wash up after the post mortem and a chipped enamel slop pail for water, blood and human remains.

I used the morgue for the first time on Halloween night in 1960. The day before Halloween, at four a.m., I received a phone call from Ingrid, a 19-year-old German immigrant. I had treated her in the past for paranoid schizophrenia.

"Hi, Doc, I just shot Lou Hudgins through the guts. I saddled my horse, roped him up and drugged him into the Horsefly River."

"You did what?"

"Yeah, Doc, he's stone cold dead. Them voices are coming back since I stopped taking my pills. They told me to shoot old Lou when he tried to get in bed with me this morning. They are telling me to do bad things. They're coming through my hair."

"Ingrid, listen closely. Unload the rifle and put it in the gun rack. Put all the lights on in the ranch house and take a couple of the pills I gave you. They are labelled largactil. I'll be out with the policeman in about an hour."

"Okay, Doc, I'm fixing to make some coffee and pluck those bad hairs out. I'll be waiting."

"Stay in the ranch house, okay?"

I called the local RCMP office and arranged for a constable and squad car to drive us out to Lou's Horsefly ranch. I picked up the emergency kit from the hospital and told the matron of our mission. Then I drove to the police station. At the station, we packed grappling hooks and waist waders for the two of us. The young constable drove to Horsefly landing with his siren blaring and his red lights flashing.

It was easy to find Horsefly Landing and a half a mile from town, we spotted the lit up ranch house. We went into the house and we both noticed that the rifle was in the single gun rack. Ingrid then showed us the imprints in the sand where she had dragged Lou to the river with her horse. Her path was easy to follow. At the edge of the river we could see the body of Lou bobbing in the current. His white long johns had caught on a log snag and glistened in the cold light of dawn.

"I'll get the waders. I can hook him with the grappling hook and land him on this gravel shore. I'll need your help pulling him in," said the constable.

Within an hour, we had Lou's body. We wrapped him in an old horse blanket on the bank. Then we waited for Joe De Geese, the mortician in Williams Lake, to come with his combination hearse and ambulance to take the body back to the morgue.

Joe finally arrived and took the body. Ingrid, the constable and I rode back to town in the squad car. At the hospital, I gave an agitated Ingrid more largactil. I made arrangements to have Ingrid go to Essondale Mental Hospital in Vancouver for treatment. I contacted the coroner and he ordered me to do an autopsy.

At seven o'clock on Halloween night, I put on my stained white post mortem coat and proceeded to autopsy Lou. I was unable to retrieve the 30.30 slug, as the wound of entrance was at the umbilicus. Lou's massive exit wound destroyed the first lumbar vertebrae in the lower back, penetrated the small and large intestines and destroyed the vena cava and aorta. I cleaned up with cold water and stumbled back on the rickety wooden walk to the warm hospital and a cup of hot coffee.

On the way back to the hospital, I could hear the wail of the kids on the streets in the cold night air, hollering, "Halloween apples."

Frances Oldham Kelsey–MD, PhD

Few Canadian physicians know that Dr. Kelsey was born in Cobble Hill on Vancouver Island in 1914. She was educated in Cobble Hill and Victoria, but moved to Montreal to study pharmacology at McGill, where she received her BSc and MSc in her chosen field of study. Later, she received a PhD and MD from the University of Chicago.

People may remember her as a Canadian crusader making a concerted effort to prevent the sale of thalidomide (kevlon) on American soil. Dr Kelsey had been hired by the U.S. Federal Drug Administration, the FDA, and she battled royally with the pharmaceutical companies over the use of this drug in the United States—due to the concerns about congenital malformations that could and did occur. She insisted that the drug should be fully tested prior to approval and sale. She had the backing of her friend and paediatric cardiologist, Dr. Helen Tausig, of Johns Hopkins Medical School. Dr. Tausig testified, in Washington, that the drug was potentially harmful if given to the mothers of America and she supported Dr. Kelsey in her decision to ban the drug in the U.S.

Dr. Kelsey was studying the effect of teratogenic drugs that caused congenital malformations at the same time I was looking after a stricken little boy. This boy's mother had been given the drug thalidomide for pregnancy-related nausea and vomiting in Cumberland County, Nova Scotia. In 1962, thalidomide was banned in Canada.

Sterling Haynes

This four-year-old, Jonathon, arrived in my office in the Cariboo region in 1962. His parents and their three kids had moved after the Springhill mine disaster in Nova Scotia. They'd bought a "stump ranch" in our Cariboo region.

This smart little guy was born with no arms and many extra toes. His biggest problem was that his jaw was locked shut and his temporo-mandibular joints were ankylosed. There was no medical scheme in British Columbia at that time and the parents had no money.

His mother and I managed to get the Shriners Children's Hospital to take Jonathon on as a patient. They took over the case completely and even paid for the transport of parents and child to and from Portland where he was treated. I looked after some of his many problems under the direction of the Shriners' plastic surgeons.

Over the years, Jonathon slowly improved until he was able to swallow and chew a little.

I remember Dr. Kelsey for having the guts and knowledge to battle suppliers of untested drugs. I believe Dr. Kelsey prevented the birth of thousands of armless and legless children.

For her great U.S. public health decisions, in 1962, she received the President's Award for Distinguished Civilian Service from President John F. Kennedy. Dr. Kelsey retired from the FDA at the age of 90 and now lives in Maryland. The Frances Kelsey Secondary School in Mill Bay, B.C. honours Dr. Kelsey's influential and instrumental role in preventing harmful drugs from being sold in the U.S., and later, banned in Canada.

"Frank" looks down the road at the Penticton, B.C. traffic circle before his fractures occurred. After his repairs he found a home at Red Rooster Winery...where an award-winning Cabernet Franc was inspired by his arrival. 1000 bottles were signed by the artist and quickly sold out in 2005.

Frank's Fractures

"Frank" was vandalized. He was, is, a work of statuesque art. He lived at the centre of a new traffic circle in Penticton, British Columbia, in front of the art gallery...oh, so long ago.

Michael Hermesh's nude sculpture, *The Baggage Handler*, made of epoxy-impregnated plaster, had both ankles broken below the calf and his genitals amputated. The twenty-four suitcases that surrounded him remained unopened, but ravaged by slashes and

97

smashes. The one bag in the statue's right hand was left somewhat intact. This work of art was first displayed January 3, 2005. He is seven feet tall and was given the nickname by art lovers.

The mayor decided that the statue was done, finished, kaput, maybe overdone—"a controversy," no less. He decreed that it would not be repaired by the city and would be placed outside city limits.

Prior to being vandalized, Pentictonites had attempted to solve the problem of Frank's nude depravity. Someone placed underwear on *The Baggage Handler* at first—his genitalia were out of view.

Another abuser pulled his shorts down to his knees. Finally, someone stuffed a *Huggie* into the genital area, perhaps to prevent accidental spills. Green paint was also smeared on the sculpture in an attempted cover up. After the last attack, urological surgeons said they could re-attach his privates and do a plastic repair on his foreskin, free of charge. Hermesh, the sculptor, could place the broken legs in plaster until things hardened and were cured.

Some local politicians were against Frank from the beginning. There had been talk that renewing the Lord's Day Alliance Act might allow him to be clothed or removed from view. Alternatively, perhaps roadblocks could be put up around the Penticton Marina to prevent people from being embarrassed while going to church. Senior Sunday drivers would not see Frank's nether regions.

A Canadian flag was found that could cover the genitals and buttocks. Bigger than a fig leaf, it just might do the trick. The maple leaf covered what a fig leaf couldn't. When the work of art was removed, in September of 2003, I think the Canadian flag should have been flown at half-mast at city hall to bring attention to Frank's departure.

A hockey buff had offered to supply an athletic metal cup from the Penticton Vees hockey team of over 50 years ago. The cup would protect and conceal the shrunken appendages of Frank. It had been proposed that a piece of steel could be fastened to erectile rebar and bolted to each buttock. The metal cup gift was returned to the potential donor and will probably end up in Penticton's hockey hall of fame, away from cheap shots.

The integrity and philosophy of Michael Hermesh's sculpture should be preserved. Perhaps the powers-that-be should have asked for an independent review or consulted with the provincial minister of culture. Later, a Royal Commission could have added their two cents worth.

Alas, now the statue has been removed. Spring flowers and shrubs will replace Frank. The old suitcases will be returned to their donors.

Frank did eventually find new lodgings and a place of respect. He now resides on the lawn of the Red Rooster Winery and visitors to the winery can enjoy the view and contemplate this creative work over a glass of wine.

I hope the director of the Art Gallery of the South Okanagan has more ideas up his sleeve. Perhaps the miniature model of Hermesh's work could be kept on display in the gallery—or bobble heads sold at the gift shop. I'm sure none if the art patrons would be offended.

"Pssst, has anyone got a band-aid?"

Sterling Haynes

Heroin

One hundred years ago, a doctor could tell his patient, "Take two heroin and see me in the morning." At that time, heroin was sold by the German pharmaceutical company, Bayer, the same company that makes aspirin today.

The word heroin is derived from the German word *heroisch*, meaning heroic. It was effective, but the prescribing doctor was audacious, not heroic. Heroin is diacetylmorphine and made from opium poppies, of which 90 percent come from Afghanistan.

Since the early 1960s, it has been illegal in Canada to be in possession of heroin—before that time, heroin was legally owned by hospitals, pharmacists and physicians.

Heroin can be a very useful drug. It is a strong cough suppressant, and an anti-diarrhoea agent used for centuries. As derivatives of heroin, paregoric is used for diarrhoea, laudanum for menstrual cramps, cough and pain relief. The downside, of course, is that heroin is strongly addictive if used daily. Samuel Taylor Coleridge, the English writer and philosopher was an opium addict. Abraham Lincoln's wife, Mary, was addicted to laudanum.

As a physician and midwife in the 1960s, I came to appreciate the effects of heroin in helping women through long labours, difficult foetal presentations and first pregnancies. Heroin reduces pain but has the power to produce a euphoric effect, described as a "body high."

In the Williams Lake region, during my time there, our rate of caesarean sections were very low—about 12 percent—as it took all three doctors and most of the nurses in this country hospital to perform the surgery and look after the baby. I prescribed heroin most days, in the case room, as I was delivering about three babies a week. In a difficult labour, intramuscular injections of about 1/12th of a grain of heroin could relax the labouring woman. It could reduce the effect of the contraction and would calm the most apprehensive young woman.

The average heroin addict shooting up uses 300 milligrams intravenously per dose, three to four times a day (about five grains). This is 60 times the dose that we ever used in the case room.

I remember one 14-year-old who came in from Horsefly Landing in labour. Ilse had had no prenatal care, spoke Low German and very little English. While she was throwing herself around in the maternity bed, I found out that she wasn't sure from which aperture the baby would exit. I could hardly believe it when I came to understand that she thought the baby would come out of her belly button.

I helped Ilse to understand that the baby would come out through the opening between her legs. The night was long and Ilse's shrieks and moans filled the little country hospital. Ilse shouted and cursed in German and broken English. After we gave her an injection of heroin, the moaning stopped and she seemed to be less anxious and more in control. I'm not sure she understood anything about the delivery of a baby.

After three or four hours of intense labour, we gave her some more heroin to help ease the pain of the contractions and she delivered the baby fairly easily. She was very pleased with herself. The postpartum ten days she spent in hospital helped her adjust to the fact that she was a mother, along with learning how to

Sterling Haynes

breastfeed her infant. She returned home to Horsefly Lake and
resumed her school studies. I never saw her again.

In 1963, the government healthcare agencies collected all
heroin from all the hospitals of the province. The medical staff in
Williams Lake decided to save five dozen tubes of heroin. Each
tube held a dozen heroin tablets; each tablet was five milligrams.
We stored this drug in the narcotic safe. Heroin was the best drug I
ever used in the case room. We had enough heroin to administer to
mothers in labour and distress for four to five more years after the
ban.

When the nurses prepared a dose of heroin for injection, the
tiny tablet was placed in a glass syringe and diluted with a sterile
fluid solution. The undissolved tablet was then heated in an alcohol
lamp until the solution was clear. Cooled, it could be injected into
the patient's buttocks.

The results in the case room were amazing–the labouring
woman became focused on the contractions and relaxed well
between pains. I think it sped labour up. Dr. Atwood and I never
had a female patient become addicted to heroin.

In my labour room cases, heroin was a "heroic" drug. I
wish it was available to women with difficult labours now. Sadly,
it is only available illegally—only to the addict and the pusher.

Sleds were the mode of transport during the difficult winter months well into the 20th century. Photo from Sage Birchwater collection.

The Freedom Road

The people of the Chilcotin Plateau are tough as jack pine knots. They come with a peculiar personality of independence, determination and self-reliance. Their home is a sparsely-populated mountain area west of the Fraser River and Williams Lake, B.C. Chilcotin residents have to be resourceful because they live on a high snowbound plateau for seven or eight months of the year. These folks, many of whom are First Nations people, are multi-talented and work as ranchers, loggers, big game guides, mechanics, bulldozer operators and road builders.

In 1923, the pioneering Bracewells made history when they settled onto their home place of 360 acres at Tatlayoka Lake in the

103

Coast Mountain range. The family's beloved Alf was born in 1924. Later, Alf Bracewell became a strong community leader, logger, rancher, cat skinner and road builder.

In 1952, the men of the West Chilcotin were determined to build the Freedom Road (Highway 20) to Bella Coola. It would run from the high Chilcotin Plateau through Tweedsmuir Park to the Pacific Ocean. The road would be a lifeline for the coastal people and the mountain ranchers and give everyone easy access to the Pacific at the port of Bella Coola, connecting them to the interior of British Columbia.

The residents enlisted the help of the people of the Bella Coola Valley to build the lower end. The total distance through the pass is 43 kilometres, or 27 miles, with grades in the steepest part at 18 percent (about a one-to-six grade). This road is dangerously steep and impassable when icy.

In 1805, Alexander Mackenzie followed the Indian Grease (Oolican) Trail when he was the first to cross North America by land. He ended up in Bella Coola. In the 1860's, gold miners used these trails to seek the gold fields at Barkerville—a hundred miles north of Williams Lake.

The Royal Engineers partially surveyed a wagon road to the Chilcotin, but the Chilcotin Indian War of 1864 stopped further roadwork. In the 1930's a government survey was done, but no roadwork was started.

During World War II, Canadian soldiers embarked on Expedition Polar Bear and surveyed a road from Anahim Lake to Bella Coola; however, it was not built because of a lack of manpower and equipment.

In 1953, the Board of Trade in the Bella Coola Valley, led by Cliff Kopas, decided they would build the road. They hired a D6 Caterpillar tractor and engineer, Elijah Gurr, to start work. Then they added a powder crew and a T18 International bulldozer and started from the bottom end of the mountain pass. The provincial government's highways department refused any more funding for the final push to complete the road to Anahim Lake, which was at the top of the pass.

The Anahim Board of Trade and the community supplied the Cat and the Cat skinner, Alf Bracewell, as well as a powder crew to complete the top end of their Freedom Road. Jerry Bracewell took an eight-millimetre movie of her husband, Alf, building the road. This documentary is available to history buffs.

After over a year of backbreaking work dynamiting rocks and clearing the road, the two Cat drivers met on September 26, 1954, an event commemorated by Mrs. Bracewell's video. Both the upper and lower road workers received very little pay for their dangerous work. That the road was completed is a tribute to the guts and pioneer determination of the local people of the West Chilcotin and the Bella Coola Valley. All supplies necessary were put on credit and billed to these dedicated men. The Social Credit party of British Columbia at that time refused to reimburse them.

Flyin' Phil Gagliardi, the flamboyant B.C. provincial minister of highways, wanted to be present for the road's opening. He arranged an entourage of vehicles for himself and local politicians.

Setting out from Williams Lake, the group was greeted by a huge sign at Alexis Creek. The sign said, "This road is not passable not even jackass-able." Many miles further on the gravel road, the entourage was faced with a detour sign which directed Flyin'

Phil's entourage into a quagmire of mud, swamp and mosquitoes close to Chilanko Forks, rather than to the new Highway 20.

After the politicians spent hours trying to get out of the mud holes, the local ranchers took pity on them and dragged the government cars out of the mud with a team of horses. They quietly removed their phony detour signs.

The politicians did make it to the grand opening of the Freedom Road. The local people had a good laugh and the story is continually retold and embellished at remote coffee shops along the route.

Seven years later, in 1960, I met Alf Bracewell when he checked in to the gray, dilapidated War Memorial Hospital early one morning. A tree had fallen across Alf's moving Cat and landed on his right collarbone. He'd driven himself to Williams Lake, about a five to six-hour ride, with his arm in a sling.

As the doctor on call, I was asked to examine his arm.

"Looks like your clavicle may be broken, Alf. There's a lot of swelling and bruising, too. Have you any numbness or loss of feeling in your right arm?"

"It was kinda numbed up at first, but I got good feeling in my arm now and good strength, too."

After determining there were no nerve or vascular injuries, I called Vi to X-ray the right shoulder and clavicle. While we were waiting, I gave Alf a combination of drugs called HMC #1 by intravenous injection. HMC was a potent drug consisting of large doses of hyoscine, morphine and carbatrol. Within minutes Alf was snoring, but he woke up while Vi took his X-rays.

The clavicle was splintered and pushed downward, but by manipulating his shoulders with my knee in his back between his shoulder blades and pulling up with my fingers around the break, I managed to reduce the fracture. Using extra-large sanitary pads to cushion each axilla and four large tensor bandages, I immobilized and held the fracture in alignment in a figure-of-eight splint. I secured the tensor bandages with giant safety pins over each of Alf's massive shoulders to give solid support.

It was after 5:30 in the morning and the hospital cooks made us a breakfast of Elk T-bone steaks, eggs, pancakes and coffee. After breakfast, Alf remarked in a laconic way.

"You know, Doc, did you mean to stick the huge safety pin through my hide? It seems to hurt worse than my fractured collar bone."

"I am so sorry. Alf, let me readjust the figure-of-eight splint and remove that dull safety pin. The nurse will give you a couple of dozen 292's for the pain; take a couple every few hours. You better have a snooze on the gurney before you head home. Be sure and see me in the office in a month or so, but leave the splint on."

After three months, the clavicle had healed well and Alf was out occasionally working on the Freedom Road with his D8 Cat and falling trees with his chainsaw or double-bitted axe. Alf's final sentence to me was, "Thanks, Doc–I'm no worse for wear and the fractures healed okay, but that's the first time I had to wear extra large sanitary pads...an' for over two months, too."

Hammy and Hector

Hammy Boucher and Hec Gillespie were hard men and superb orthopaedic surgeons. They were the antitheses of each other.

Hammy, a tall powerfully-built man, was stern, and sometimes distant. He ate interns and residents at Vancouver General Hospital and Shaughnessy Veteran Hospital every morning for breakfast. To Hammy, orthopaedic surgery was no joking matter.

Hec was an affable, chunky man, a good teacher, with a great bedside manner. He was also the doctor for the B.C. Lions professional football team.

Both men had perfected the "no touch technique" used in the surgical theatre. During all procedures, they only handled tissue and bone with sterile instruments. This method was very difficult to learn by junior residents who didn't have powerful hands. Jokesters say an orthopaedic surgeon has to be strong as an ox and twice as smart. Both these men were strong and very intelligent, medically and mentally.

In 1959, Hammy devised and perfected a procedure called the Boucher Fusion, which was a transluminar screw fixation of the pedicles of the lumbar and sacral spine. The procedure was innovative and hastened early recovery when a back fusion was necessary. The procedure is still being used today.

As a general practitioner in Williams Lake, I referred most of my difficult cases to Hammy or Hec.

In May, 1961, I was called to go to One-Eye Lake in the Chilcotin region, a few miles from the Puntzi U.S. Air Force Base.

A light plane had crashed with three people aboard and Cappy Lloyd, the radio-telephone operator at the One-Eye Lake Lodge, told me to get to the wreck immediately. I gathered my bag of Thomas splints, yards of bandaging and dressings and ten litres of IV fluids. Soon I was at the dock by Colonel Joe's float plane on Williams Lake. Joe, a Southerner, had been a U.S. fighter pilot on the Burma Road in World War II. When I got to the dock, Joe was gassing up his Cessna 180 by hand from a 45-gallon drum of high-octane fuel.

"What do ya know good, Doc? Don't want to hear no troubles—jist give me the positives," said Joe. "Here, I'll help load your stuff in, then we'll be off like a dirty shirt."

Once we were in the air, Joe asked me to find the section of the maps that showed One-Eye Lake. I searched the back of the plane but that topographical map section was gone. In the hazy smoke from forest fires we searched, flying at 300 feet west of the Puntzi Moutain Airbase until we heard and saw a man on a small lake firing shotgun shells. It was Cappy. He waved us in and we landed on the lake.

With the U.S. sergeant medic, a PFC soldier from Puntzi Mountain and two young First Nations lads, we set down the trail with Cappy in the lead. We walked about half a mile and heard screaming. Then we saw the front end and the propeller of the crashed plane buried in the mud. I was first one there and the boys followed with all the medical equipment. The sergeant carried the Thomas splints and mesh metal stretcher.

Sterling Haynes

I managed to pry open the door and found the pilot, Jack...dead. Kenny Huston was still strapped in the co-pilot's seat and Jack's teenage son was sitting on sleeping bags at the back of the plane in shock, nursing his ankle. Kenny's scalp was on the dashboard. I remember throwing Kenny's bagged tomato sandwich on the floor and stuffing his scalp in the brown bag. I placed the bagged scalp into my pocket.

All five of us managed to gently get Kenny onto the padded metal wire stretcher and I placed one leg in a Thomas splint for his badly fractured femur. Then I threaded two intra-catheters into the veins of his broken arms. The two young men carried the bottles of saline now attached to Kenny's veins. Cappy assisted the young lad out of the plane and helped him hobble back to the lodge.

We started carrying Kenny, but a few hundred yards along the trail, he stopped breathing. I intubated him on the muddy path. Then his stertorous breathing reassured me as we carried him along the swampy lakeshore. While we were away, Colonel Joe had gassed up the plane in anticipation of flying the injured parties back to Williams Lake.

"Doc, what say we strap Kenny to one of the pontoons? We don't have room in my plane."

"Colonel Joe, are you out of your mind? I'll get the RCMP's large Beaver aircraft to fly down from Prince George. When you get back to Williams Lake notify the hospital matron, Doreen Campbell, of our problems. We'll be back in three or four hours."

Back in Williams Lake, Dr. John Hunt and I splinted some of Kenny's 43 fractures and transfused him with six units of blood.

110

I retrieved the scalp from the brown sandwich bag and re-attached it with many stitches.

At dawn the next day, Kenny was transferred via the Air-Sea Rescue's Grumman flying boat to the Richmond docks and then to Vancouver General Hospital under the care of Hammy. Kenny was to remain a patient there for three years.

Kenny returned to town with no crutches and later married Doreen Campbell, the hospital matron.

Over 40 years later, I was in the Williams Lake library reading some of my stories at one of my book launches. At the end of the evening, Kenny Huston came up to me to talk and buy my book, *Bloody Practice*.

"Ya know, Doc, my life in Williams Lake has been great since the accident. Doreen and I have good kids and many grandkids, too. My hair has grown back in and we are very happy."

"Congratulations, Kenny," I answered, "we know that two things are working well and let me feel the scar on your scalp. My gosh, I can hardly feel the ridge now. Please show me a picture of your family. Great photo, Kenny, what a man!"

Sterling Haynes

The Jelly Belly Blues

Some time ago, I got the Norwalk virus and started vomiting. Dr. Sean and the happy band of emergency room nurses at the Kelowna General Hospital stopped my vomiting and rehydrated me with fluids intravenously. During my uncontrollable bout of throwing up, my small umbilical hernia had split and become enlarged, resulting in a large abdominal defect that needed to be fixed by a surgeon.

Dr. Bernie, my GP, recommended a surgeon I'll call Dr. K. Off I went to see him about getting the hernia repaired. He looked at my midsection, including my belly button. My "innie" had now become an "outie." The good doc exhorted me to lose 25 pounds before the surgery.

I sought help at the Weight Watchers International office in West Kelowna, where the attractive women told me the program could help reduce my belly. I was hoping to have a direct line to Fergie, the ex-royal princess, but, alas, she was only a figurehead—my case would be handled by local beauties.

The weight came off in dibs and dabs and my belly profile improved. I managed to reduce my second double chin as an added bonus. I had grandiose dreams of placing a diamond in my belly button after my hernia repair.

On the initial visit to my surgeon, he showed me a large mesh net. This resembled the cod end of a trawl or the narrow end of a fish landing net. Luckily, there were no knots holding my fish net together. It looked strong. My hernia was to be netted, like a big sucker, which would prevent fat from breaking through onto the inside of my shirt and giving it a grease stain. This was to be done surgically under local anaesthesia.

Dr. K said he would be producer and director, using some high-tech equipment. He would use a 27-inch TV screen to view my belly button defect, and a fibre-optic scope to tuck and put the net into place. I was assured there would be "no scars."

"What about the old *vest-over pants* surgical procedure that used to be done 40 years ago to repair large umbilical and incisional hernias?" I asked. It was a fashionable tummy tuck with no bulges. The vest would cover the pants.

"That type of procedure puts abdominal muscles under undue stress and prolongs the recovery phase. At times, these types of hernias could recur. *Vest-over pants* is archaic; older surgeons still do this procedure. It is a repair that will disappear like the dinosaur," said the surgeon.

At first, I wondered if he was referring to me as an old dinosaur. Dr. K seemed like such a pleasant, laconic young man that I immediately put this thought out of my mind.

At the end of the consultation, the office clerk told me that the Kelowna General Hospital booking officer would let me know when it would be convenient for them to arrange the surgery. There was no need to call Dr. K again. I was given a list of instructions to follow before my surgery. It was cut and dried, so to speak.

About two months later, I received a late evening call asking me if I would fill in for a patient. He'd just been involved in a head-on collision and was unable to keep his appointment. I pondered for a few seconds then said, "Thank you very much, I'll be glad to take his place." After I hung up the phone, a multitude of thoughts flooded my brain, including the wisdom of agreeing, but it was too late. I told myself I was a lucky guy–what could go wrong?

I arrived at the Kelowna General Hospital at seven that morning. The clerk directing me to the outpatient surgical suite couldn't find my name on the booking sheet at first. Finally, on the last sheet she found my name. The original name had been crossed out and my name penciled over it—I was lucky. In red ink, the word *died* had been written over the man's name. I was the dead man's replacement. Was I a dead man walking now?

A very pleasant nurse greeted me in the operative suite and told me to take all my clothes off but to leave my socks on. I was given a short white gown with the broken off string ties at the back. The gown would have fit a small woman, not a slimmed down heavyweight man. I did manage to tie the gown's top string to the bottom third string on the opposite side. I hung my clothes up on the change room door and modestly made my appearance.

The nurse greeted me by saying, "My goodness, you look lop-sided from the rear." I felt lop-sided and tried to cover my butt with the flimsy piece of white cloth.

"Not to worry," she said. "We're all used to seeing things like this."

"Things like what?" I said as I cupped my genitals with my hands.

"Never mind, we'll hook you up to the monitor and start an IV. We have a second-year nursing student with us this morning and she's never put an intracath-canula into anyone's vein before.

Your veins look very good. I told her she only gets three tries on you and then I take over."

"Three tries?" I asked, scratching my genitals.

The shy, attractive young student moved in and wished me a good morning. She picked up the plastic intra-catheter, but then seemed unsure of what to do next.

"There's a big vein on his left forearm. Be deliberate and bold. You can't miss. It's as big as a pencil. Make a fist please, sir, as I put the tourniquet on."

The student nurse made a few tentative jabs.

"Come on, don't be chicken," her mentor said.

"Yes, don't be chicken," I echoed.

The young student finally inserted the catheter into my vein. The nurse and my old friend, Gary, on the next stretcher, cheered. Gary was to follow me and have his hernia netted. The young nurse blushed and smiled.

I chuckled at Gary. He was to be the student nurse's next victim. I told Gary that I was pulling for him and was ready to cheer the young nurse when the IV was running. If he didn't flinch I'd buy him a beer when we'd both recovered. We could compare our bellies. Gary didn't flinch and, after a few tries, the IV was running. We said our goodbyes.

The nurse gave me a green cap to put on. It was colour-coordinated to match my rust-coloured socks. Then I was wheeled into the operating theatre where everyone had green hats, green scrub suits and white masks. A disembodied male voice asked how I was doing.

"Is that you, Dr. K?" It was. "Yes, I'm okay. 'As well as can be expected,' to coin a hospital phrase," I said.

"Now I'll give a little anaesthetic through your IV tubing. When you wake up, the mesh will have been tucked into the whole defect. You'll be a new man with a strong abdominal wall. Come back and see me in two months after surgery. If you have problems contact your doctor. I'll leave a prescription at the nurses' station. You may have a little pain tonight. Remember no lifting of any weight more than 20 pounds for six weeks."

The procedure went well and I left the hospital before noon the next day. After retrieving my clothes and dressing in the small women's toilet, I exited, slightly bent over. I got the strangest look from a prim-looking young woman.

"Sorry, Ma'am, but I was told to undress and then dress in the women's toilet. I think the hospital is short of space. Hope you weren't waiting long. I'm moving slowly, just had abdominal surgery."

She looked at me quizzically, then rushed into the cubicle and slammed the door. Slowly, I left the outpatient surgical suite and found my way out of the maze of departments. I had left my cheap Timex watch on the back of the toilet, but nothing could induce me to retrieve it. With my wife leading the way, we managed to find our way amidst piles of dirty laundry stacked in canvas rolling bins in the basement corridors.

Luckily, the parking meter still had ten minutes left. The anaesthetic was starting to wear off when I picked up the Tylenol 3 from the pharmacy. I made it back to my bed with a hot water bottle and noticed a little bleeding on my dressing as I downed a couple of pain pills. My abdominal wall felt solid and meshed.

Over the next few days, I bled a little from my navel. A dark stain marked my underwear and at times my T-shirt. The tape used to hold the modest dressing was irritating my skin. After a particularly heavy red stain marked my pants, shirt and underwear, I ripped off the tape as well as hair and a half-inch piece of my hide. I was now scarred from the adhesive on either side of my belly button. Dr. K was wrong—there would be a scar.

After two weeks, I developed a swelling around my navel that grew in size. There was a large amount of bruising that extended south to my genitals and settled in my scrotum. I went back to my GP and he referred me back to the surgeon. Dr. K told me that the hematoma would drain slowly and the swelling would be gone by the time the draining stopped.

"See me at the end of August in my office," he said breezily.

I agreed to wipe off the red currant gel from my belly's jelly, take a hot shower each morning and get rid of the clots with pressure.

Doc K was right; with the correct routine, the ooze and clots left my belly button. My daughters suggested that I have a tattoo placed around my belly button. They thought of a number of tattoos. An anchor might weigh me down, but as I was a retired doctor, they thought a caduceus, the symbol of medicine, might fit the bill. It could promote my healing innie as I adopted the Buddha position for navel contemplation.

Sterling Haynes

With further weight loss, perhaps I would gather enough courage to go to beaches wearing a thong. My abs, glutes, pecs would be solid after a bit of weight loss. Perhaps a few sessions in the weight room at Gold's Gym would make me an Adonis. A flat belly and a few testosterone patches might restore my vigour. I could be a born-again. I would be a Greek god in the body of Arnold Schwarzenegger—in my fantasy.

A few days in the gym convinced me that the surgeon might change my body, but I wasn't motivated to change my shape.

Perhaps I could show off my flat belly button with hipster jeans and a tank top. My wife didn't think that this was a good idea for a 77-year-old man. I'm now wearing baggie sweat pants and a sweat shirt accessorizing my old boy Biggar, Saskatchewan hat.

Occasionally, I drop in at a Weight Watchers meeting to see the svelte women and win a silver star when I lose five pounds in a week.

I'm looking forward to getting into my silk pants with a 40-inch waist. I hum a little tune, do a little jig and improvise some of my lyrics to a reggae beat.

I had the jelly belly button blues
blue as they can be.
Now, I'm a new man, Mister
and flat as you can see.
The belly button blues.
Done gone south, Sister.
They's all left me
And taken off for Tennessee.

Meeting On The Road

Ginnie died in February a few years ago. I didn't know her well, but we met in unusual circumstances over 40 years ago.

My wife and I had been shooting blue grouse on the Chilcotin Plateau in central British Columbia. The back of the station wagon was loaded with dead blue and sharp-tailed grouse we'd shot on Beecher's Prairie. Our Brittany Spaniel, Beau, lay dreaming and exhausted on the back seat. We were dirty from the week's hunt. Our hosts at the shooting lodge had given us a huge breakfast of steak, beans and hot fruit salad that had been brewing in brandy at the back of the wooden cook stove. We were primed for the day.

We left Riske Creek Lodge with a tank full of gas. We had a long journey ahead, much of it through the Gang Ranch on a remote gravel road. It would be many miles after we crossed the Fraser River before we would hit paved highways and our home in Kamloops. I looked forward to the countryside, the hills dressed in fall colours.

By mid-afternoon, we were driving down a steep bank to the Fraser River, which we crossed on a single lane wooden bridge built by the Royal Corps of Engineers a hundred years ago. We drove slowly as the mighty Fraser River's boiling rapids rumbled below us. The water shot through the entrance to Hell's Gate. On the steep incline on the other side, we saw a woman. She flagged us down. She was the driver of a large Land Rover truck with

119

trailer. I could see she had a flat tire. We parked our car behind the trailer.

"My name is Ginnie," she said. "My husband, Rand, and ten Scottish soldiers under his command are attempting to travel down the Fraser River in rubber rafts. I'm carrying supplies for the group from station to station. I'm late for my rendezvous with the men at Big Bar, a few miles downstream. I'll need help changing this tire."

"Sure, we'll help. This is my wife, Jessie, and my name is Sterling."

We shook hands and she gave me her card. I found my card and gave it to her. She was dressed in English army clothes. I explained, "I'm a doctor and my wife and I are returning home from a week of bird shooting. It looks like this tire changing is going to be a big job. Should be finished before dusk."

The spare tire was bolted to the top of the hood. The nuts were rusted on. I tried to turn the nuts with the tire rod. I managed to loosen one, but bent the tire rod. Luckily, Ginnie found a pipe wrench and a piece of lead pipe that fit on to the handle. With many oaths, I managed to unscrew the nuts. Ginnie offered me tea from a thermos. It was hot and sweet and gave me strength to tackle the nuts on the flat tire. There were six tremendous screeches before I loosened them.

The spare tire was very heavy, but we managed to wrestle it off the bonnet and roll it to the flat. I got the jack under the axle, but barely lifted the truck high enough to get the flat tire off. Then I had to dig a hole under the tire to give me enough room to pull the brute off. By this time I was sweating and much dirtier. I managed to lift the spare, and squatting, I got the tire balanced on the rim of the axle. Suddenly, the seat of my pants ripped and I passed a thunderous sound of music. Feeling mortified, I kept my eyes down. I could feel my face reddening.

The sound was unexpected; it seemed to reverberate in the stillness of the Coast Mountains. I looked up and the two women were convulsing with laughter; I grinned and started to laugh with them.

Three hours later, Ginnie thanked us as we tidied up. She started up her lorry and slowly crawled up the hill. At the top of the hill, we waved goodbye as we passed one another.

When I returned home, I later researched the life of Virginia and Sir Ranulph Fiennes and the Nahanni River Expedition in Canada's north. Sir Rand was writing a book called *The Headless Valley* and was going to include a tale of their adventures through Hell's Gate on the Fraser River.

Three weeks later in my clinic office, I received an official embossed card thanking us for our help on the road. The noisy incident was not mentioned. Ginnie said her husband would make note of our help in his writings. Under her official British coat-of-arms, she signed the card, Lady Virginia Twistleton-Wykheham-Fiennes.

Lady Virginia Fiennes was the first woman awarded the Polar Medal. The medal was bestowed on her by the Queen of England to honour her exploits at both poles of the earth. One could say she was bi-polar.

Sir Ranulph Fiennes was awarded the Order of the British Empire (OBE) for over 30 explorations and discoveries. His 52,000-mile trans-global expedition took three years to complete.

Later, he and his partners discovered the lost city of Ubar in the Rub Al desert of Oman. These two major exploits prompted Prince Charles of England to label Sir Rand as "mad but marvellous" and the *Guinness Book of Records* named him "the world's greatest living explorer."

Onan, The Bull

In British Columbia, many Cariboo ranchers say that one bull is 50 percent of a herd. After treating a Hereford bull with a broken foreleg, I would say one bull is more a majority of a herd.

On a cold February in 1963, on a Tuesday afternoon, my friend John, a Williams Lake veterinarian, asked me, a GP anaesthetist, if I could give an anaesthetic to a prize bull with a broken leg. The bull was in a paddock south of "the Lake" in central British Columbia. This animal, in its prime, had become entangled in a few old strands of barbed wire. Then it had fallen and broken its foreleg. The wire was still wound around the leg and the bull was mad. The owner had named the bull Onan, a dastardly character from biblical times. The mounted cowboys were very scared of this large horny animal.

The ranch owner was a God-fearing Baptist from Texas. He had taken the name Onan from Genesis 38:9. This biblical man went to be with his brother's wife one night and he, like the bull in the pasture, spilled his seed upon the ground. This active bull had carelessly serviced 60 cows in November before he broke his leg. This was one raunchy bull with a badly broken leg.

John had been informed that the paddock was close to the San Jose River, known among the Cariboo-ites as the San Josey River. Luckily, there was a large snubbing post in the center of the field beside the water.

John drove us out to the ranch in his Land Rover. We were loaded for bull. Arriving at the ranch house, we parked next to a new pink Cadillac. The owner met us with, "Hi y'all. Doing all right? Just call me Tex. That there Onan is worked up some. Most

123

Sterling Haynes

of the boys stay clear of him, me included. It looks like his right foreleg is busted, cain't even get the barbwire off o' his leg—he's a mess."

Dr. John had dealings before with this ranch owner. He said, "I'll need at least three cowboys, your best ropers with their best horses. We can't operate on Onan's leg without good help, you understand?"

"No need to get to get uppity about it, Doc. My best boys will give you a hand—that's for damn sure. The bull is in the paddock north of the barn by the snubbing post. Boys, show the doc the way."

"Thanks, Tex. You must be doing well. I like your new pink Cadillac."
Photo from Sage Birchwater collection.

A sample of the work these cowboys participated in on the ranches. Marvin Curtis was photographed here in 1924. Rodeos were a mainstay of the recreational side of Chilcotin life. Williams Lake was a major hub for this event.

Where Does It Hurt Now?

We followed the three cowboys and their mounts to the pasture. There was Onan standing on three legs, bellowing. We could see the barbed wire entanglement and the angled broken radius of the foreleg.

"Now listen carefully, you men," said John. "I want three lariats to lasso the bull. The one around the neck is to be snubbed to the snubbing post. The other two are be secured—one around each hind leg and the slack taken up and the rope secured to your saddle horns.

"Your job is to spread out the bull, but don't put him down. I have large, soft cotton ropes that I'll secure to the neck and the three undamaged legs. These soft ropes will be used to pull him down after he has a little anaesthetic."

"We understand, Doc," said the foreman.

"Now, I'll need four pails of clean water to wash in along with washing the bull's leg. I'll need a pair of fencing pliers to get the barbed wire off. My Coleman stove's flame will be used to sterilize the steel rod. Understand, boys?"

"We's got it, Doc."

It was to be a long, cold afternoon. The three cowboys managed to get the lariats around the bull's neck and his hind legs. With a great deal of swearing and cajoling, the animal was strung out from the large snubbing post as two of the ropes were fastened around saddle horns. Then John and I used the large, soft ropes to doubly secure the animal and get it down on the large white tarps we had placed around the hitching post.

The Coleman stove was started and the veterinary instruments boiled in a pail. The intramedullary steel rod was sterilized by flame and left to cool on the stove. With Dr. John's precise instruction, I mixed up a solution of chloral hydrate in a gallon of sterile water. My garden hose was ready to be used as an endotracheal tube. A bent garden fork had been fashioned into a McIntosh laryngoscope, sort of. We further snubbed the bull's neck to the post. I was poised with my number eight needle by a huge jugular vein. The bull's bellows were awesome.

Whap. I shoved the sharp end of the needle into the vein. Then I started the drip of chloral hydrate solution through this huge vein. As the bull became groggy, all five us gradually lowered the massive beast onto the clean canvas. It was a struggle. John had taken off his parka and shirt. He now wore a sleeveless fleece vest. He washed his hands and huge arms in a chloride of lime solution and antiseptic soap. He had everything in readiness.

.

With much difficulty, I finally managed to get the endotracheal garden hose through the bull's larynx as the cowboys extended its neck by pulling on the horns. We were ready.

With the broken foreleg raised higher than the rest of Onan, John clipped the barbwire, then scrubbed and paired away part of the hoof. He lined up the fractured radius manually. Giant lion jaw orthopaedic clamps held the fractured ends. With John's alacrity and skill, the sterilized intramedullary rod was hammered carefully up the broken radius shaft. The fracture appeared solid. The wounds were sutured and closed. A massive dressing smeared with antibiotic ointment was applied under a sleeve of cowhide and tied in place with binder twine.

Then, the bull started to wake up.

I removed the IV as we prodded and pulled the animal to its feet with the help of the horses. The beast was a bit groggy as it awakened, but the bellowing stopped. The animal seemed content to stand on his three good legs. With the fracture reduced, Onan the bull seemed pain free in his recovery space.

I got a little careless at the end of the arduous procedure and managed to catch a few splatterings from a shower of bull s*#t as I packed up my garden hose, pail and modified garden spade, my homemade laryngoscope.

We were shivering as we drove back to the ranch house. There was no mention of even a cup of coffee or thanks from the Texan.

"That bull should be okay now but I'll keep checking," said John. "Keep him in a clean stall with clean bedding straw. That will be a hundred dollars, Tex, please."

"Well, I don't have a hundred bucks, Doc."

"You better get it, Tex. And right now! Have you ever seen how these diabolical little clamps work for gelding stallions? I can place two clamps, just like these, in one minute, Tex, guaranteed."

Tex opened his wallet and placed a crisp new hundred dollar bill into John's massive hand.

Typical cabin of the Chilcotin people in early 20ᵗʰ century from the Sage Birchwater collection.

Nola Belle

I'd known Nola Belle all her life, since I had delivered her.

In 1964, Nola was a sweet four-year-old who lived on a ranch along the Dog Creek Road, twelve miles west of Williams Lake. Nola was small but sturdy, a pretty girl with big brown eyes and black hair. She loved her kitties and her horse, Betsy, and liked to play with her animals.

It was the Friday before Thanksgiving when Nola Belle began to feel ill. Nola watched her brother and sister get on the school bus and then complained to her mother.

"Mommy, I feel sick."

Nola Belle never spoke another word. She started coughing continually. Within an hour, she was struggling to breathe. Her mom loaded her into the pickup and drove as fast as she could to the Cariboo Memorial Hospital in town.

When I saw Nola Belle, four hours later, her lips were blue, her chest was indrawn and when she breathed her whole thorax caved in with rapid respirations.

The charge nurse, Iris Campbell, started oxygen. Vi Clarke, our X-ray technician, took chest X-rays. I placed a cut down in a vein of Nola's left ankle and threaded a plastic tube into the leg vein and sutured it there. Then I started intravenous chloramphenicol and penicillin and injected streptomycin into her buttock.

Sol Raj, the medical technologist, took sputum samples for cultures and gram-stained the slide for bacteria. Within an hour, the hospital staff realized that Nola Belle had a fulminating Staphylococcal pneumonia and likely the dreaded staph septicaemia.

I called my partner, Dr. Hugh Atwood, to help. The Williams Lake Hospital didn't have a ventilator at this time. I intubated Nola Belle and, with Hughie's assistance, we ventilated her artificially with an Ambu rubber bag and oxygen. Slowly over the next 12 hours, it became increasingly difficult to ventilate Nola Belle as she became less responsive. Her lungs were filling up with pus and Staph toxins despite the antibiotics and large doses of intravenous hydrocortisone we'd given her.

About midnight, Nola Belle's pupils became fixed and dilated. Dr. Atwood and I, along with her mother and father, decided that Nola Belle could never recover.

129

Sterling Haynes

We stopped ventilating the sweet little girl.

A few days later the blood cultures results came back from the lab. All six cultures were coagulase positive and grew the virulent Staphylococcus aureus. Nowadays, the medical term for her death would be a Cytokine Storm. For her parents, Dr. Hugh and me, her death was a nightmare.

During the crisis, the family said little, but later, many tears were shed for Nola. I spent that Thanksgiving weekend walking in the woods. I couldn't work. Visions of Nola Belle dying would be with me forever. She was the first young child who died under my care.

The family never blamed me and I didn't feel any resentment from them. They continued to see me over the years for their medical problems. The memory, however, of that vulnerable little girl dying before my eyes is still there, 55 years later, like a deep scratch on a mirror.

Peyote Pictures

The peyote plant is a divine cactus. It is small, without thorns, and shaped like a dumpling. This plant, *Lophophora williamsii*, grows wild in the warm desert regions of the Americas, but can be easily cultivated indoors anywhere. Aboriginal people harvest and dry the top and the flowers for religious use. Peyote produces a hallucinogenic substance called mescaline.

Mescaline may be eaten in its button form or drunk as a bitter liquid. To the spiritual groups of the aboriginal people, the shaman of the tribe usually administers the drug. In many of the states of the U.S., it is illegal to possess or traffic in peyote. In Canada, peyote is legal and is used by local First Nations people in religious ceremonies, particularly on the Blood and Blackfoot reserves in southern Alberta.

The Huichol of Mexico use peyote in religious ceremonies to inspire their members to produce magnificent paintings and sculpture. These descendants of the Aztecs are great artists—they ingest peyote to induce brilliant kaleidoscopic visions. They then portray their hallucinations. Using resins and beeswax, they glue the yarn onto the backs of various sizes of plywood.

The usual peyote dose ingested is 29 mescal buttons, equivalent to 300-600 milligrams of pure mescaline. It is this dose that produces visual hallucinations. The mescal buttons may be eaten or dissolved in Coca-Cola to mask the very bitter taste. The peyote causes an intensification of colours and marvellous changes in textures of objects and shapes. The hallucinations last up to several hours. The drug's side effects may be nausea and vomiting. The shamans consider vomiting to be a type of body cleansing.

Sterling Haynes

Occasionally, the user may experience uncontrollable laughter, dizziness, rapid heart rate, anxiety and other transient symptoms.

I became interested in Huichol pictures inspired by peyote while on art walks through Puerto Vallarta and surrounding towns. The vibrant wool drawings displayed in the shops of the glass bead artists and carvers attracted our attention. We were determined to visit an artistic Huichol community.

Our Spanish-speaking daughter, Elizabeth, my wife, Jessie and I embarked on a four-hour bus journey north and east from Puerto Vallarta to a remote village in the foothills of the Sierra Madre. The last portion, on gravel and cobblestone single-lane roads, jolted us as we climbed higher and higher on a switchback trail. Eventually we reached this village that contained a newly-constructed primary bilingual school (Huichol–Spanish) and a small government-sponsored cooperative store.

As we walked through the settlement, our Mexican guide, Miguel, told us that many Huichol people over the age of 30 did not speak Spanish due to their isolation from Mexican society. Many still believed the earth was flat.

We watched the yarn painters cover their prepared wooden surface with a mixture of beeswax and pine resin. Then they used beads or wool thread and attached them to the wax-resin mixture to make their designs. The results were breathtaking vibrant reds and yellows woven into a panorama surrounding the eight-lobed flower of the peyote cactus. I purchased a painting done by Amalia Evangelista, an 18-year-old student at a local college, for one daughter's birthday. On the back of the plywood picture, she described what her visions were and how her wool painting depicted them.

Here is the English translation:

"The picture represents the big peyote, different from the rest because this peyote is a more sacred more powerful one because it has more magical power. This is why the standing clouds are throwing snakes to protect the offerings from the gods. Also represented is a *jicara* (a Mexican gourd) filled with offerings and a drum. Let the party begin!"

Next, Miguel and the shaman led us to their church. The shamans wore bleached cotton pants and cotton tunics embroidered with colourful designs of flowers and animals. Their brimmed hats were decorated with feathers and many small shells were also attached to each hat.

At the adobe church entrance, Miguel asked us to observe and honour a small heaped collection—an offering of the head of a recently killed four-point white-tailed deer, a potted peyote plant, a primitive bow and four small metal-tipped arrows. Small wooden sticks were adorned with a variety of feathers and placed around the edges of the display. The feathers are, we were told, to cleanse our spirits before we enter their ceremonial building. We walked with care around the attending shaman's spiritual display before we proceeded inside.

The Huichols have taken some of the teachings of their Roman Catholic neighbours and woven them into their religious beliefs. On the mantel inside the church on the far wall was a large portrait of the Catholic saint, the Virgin of Guadalupe. Next to this central figure were bows and sacred arrows, more feathers, antlers and a very large ammonite fossil. The collection of objects and the shaman's talk were very provocative and seemed to take us back in time to a more ancient America.

Sterling Haynes

Walking back to the bus, I looked at the small houses with their fenced backyards containing chickens, skinny, small short-haired dogs, goats and open pit toilets. I wondered about the health conditions of the children. I did notice that the rainwater barrels seemed clear and clean. There was a large new concrete tank supplying water to the government store.

The bus journey back on the narrow cobblestone road was slowed when we were forced to the side to allow a large red truck to pass. It was grinding its way up to the store. As it squeezed passed us, I noticed the Coca-Cola logo painted on the side. Emblazoned in Spanish as well on the back of the lorry was *Siempre Coke*—Always Coke.

Perhaps things do "go better with Coke," especially when taken with peyote.

A family camp for the Chilcotin. This shot was taken circa 1920 and is from Sage Birchwater collection.

A Woman on a Mission

Sister Theresa was a gem: compassionate and dedicated to people and her calling.

She was a Grey nun and a registered nurse who looked after the people of the Cariboo in central British Columbia from the 1950's to the 60's. She lived in the Roman Catholic Mission at Alexis Creek and at times would come to Williams Lake and stay at the Catholic Mission on the Sugar Cane Reserve just outside of town.

Sterling Haynes

For years, this woman never took a day off. She looked after all the people of the remote Chilcotin, but especially the Chilcotin and Carrier peoples from the Ulkatcho Mountains— along with the Toosey Band at Riske Creek. These people lived in remote areas, miles apart. This nursing sister brought the sick and maimed to the Alexis Creek Red Cross Outpost Hospital or the War Memorial Hospital in Williams Lake.

She drove her beat up Ford van along the dusty, corduroy roads to Anahim Lake, Nemiah Valley and all the isolated reserves in the Chilcotin, returning to the hospitals at Alexis Creek and "the Lake," as needed. In the winter, she put the chains on the van and drove to isolated reserves. She was physically strong and had a mental toughness that was hard to match.

I loved her as a nun should be loved—with all my heart. To me, she was a saint, even though I'm not Catholic.

Sister Theresa was a sturdy woman. Her wimple was not always completely white. Her face, hands and arms were always tanned from the sun and the wind. Her arms were muscular from changing tires or putting chains on her tires in forty below temperatures—she was ready to go anywhere, at any time, especially if there was a medical emergency.

I first met Sister Theresa during the Williams Lake Stampede in the 1960's. The covered wagons from Nemiah Valley and the Ulkatcho Mountains were drawn by Pinto Cayuse horses. The First Nations people came with families filling the wagons and their trailing horses tied behind the primitive transports. Their talented cowboys were ever eager to ride in the stampede and show their prowess.

The Chilcotins watered their stock in the upper reaches of Riske Creek before heading downhill to cross the Fraser River and enter the stampede fairgrounds. In the spring and summer of every year, Riske Creek's water at the top of Sheep Creek Hill was the source of *Shigella dysenteriae*. Babies in their moose hide cradles seemed to be particularly prone to it. Many died and were placed under rocks beside the trail on the way to town. Sister Theresa spent a lot of time teaching the families the benefits of boiling their drinking water.

Often the camping grounds had epidemics of severe diarrhoea caused by the bacteria, *Shigellosis*. The babies vomited and could quickly become severely dehydrated. In the early days of my practice, these epidemics were labelled "summer complaint" by health care workers.

Sister Theresa monitored these infants at the fairgrounds and, if they became dehydrated, brought them to the old War Memorial Hospital for treatment. Usually my partner, Dr. Donald McLean, and I—the two junior medical practitioners—were appointed by the older doctors to be on call during Stampede week.

One day, I got a phone call from Donald.

"Come quickly, Sterling, Sister Theresa has just brought in two babies from the Indian camp on the Stampede grounds. I have never seen such sick babies before—not even as a student in Edinburgh. They may die!"

"I'll be right down." I answered. "Please ask Nurse Campbell to get the cut-down trays out. We are probably in for an epidemic. There is limited potable water and poor sewage disposal in crowded tents and wagons. Sister Theresa will be patrolling the campgrounds: there'll be more to come."

"Should I phone Dr. Fraser?" Donald asked about the federal government administrator for the Department of Indian Affairs.

"No, don't bother now. Phone him tomorrow. He'll send a public health nurse out to the Toosey Band at Riske Creek tomorrow to warn the people to boil their water during this epidemic."

I arrived at the emergency room to find the babies. At that time, the local hospital did not do the flame photometry test for serum electrolytes. Sol Raj, the medtech, did the basic haematology, urinalysis and BUNs (blood urea nitrogen). The BUNs were all elevated indicating impending renal failure and body acidosis from dehydration. We had to work fast to rehydrate and replace the serum sodium, potassium and chloride electrolytes.

I greeted one of the mothers.

"Hi, Mrs. Charleyboy. I see you got a very sick boy. Willie, isn't it? I delivered him here about ten months ago, in September, right?"

"Yeah, Doc, Willie was a big guy but not anymore. He's my only boy. He's got the shitters now and been vomiting since we left Riske Creek. He looks like an ole prune, Doc. He don't even cry now, not even a whimper."

"We'll try our best, Mrs. Charleyboy. He'll have to stay here in hospital. He's very sick."

"I know he is, Doc. Please do everything you can."

In the emergency room, Donald and I placed cut downs, plastic tubes, in the large saphenous veins of the babies' ankles. First, we ran a litre of normal saline through each child's vein, then salt and then added sugar water. We assessed the children every three to four hours. The kids went from looking like old shoes to vibrant black-eyed plums. Within two days, they were taking apple juice, weak tea and then bananas. Slowly, their urinary output increased.

By mid-summer that year, the hospital was full of recovered babies. But the parents and their covered wagons had moved to Farwell Canyon to start the salmon fishing along the Chilko River. They knew their babies were in safe hands.

Photo of a Chilcotin fishing camp from the Sage Birchwater collection.

The deejays would announce over the local radio for the Charleyboy family, or the Quilts, or the Desters to pick up their kids. The Department of Indian Affairs were informed by the hospital of the need for their beds. Finally, Sister Theresa came with her Ford van, loaded up the kids and took them back home to their loving grandparents on the reserves.

A few years later, she was recalled to a nunnery by the Bishop of Quebec and asked to renew her vows to God in Montreal. I never saw her again.

I missed her enthusiasm, intellect, savvy, practicality and dedication. She was a diamond in the rough, a pure joy to work with. I wish I'd been able to tell her the results of her work, how those babies she saved grew up to be miners, farmers, teachers and rodeo riders.

A Chilcotin family lines the family home. Photo from the Sage Birchwater collection.

Stew

Stewart Burris was delivered with the help of his uncle in 1920 at the Royal Inland Hospital in Kamloops, B.C. His dad, always known as H.L., was a physician, too.

I found H. L. to be a very reasonable and easy-going fellow. Stewart's mother, Robina, was a gem from Manitoba who always had a positive outlook. She was well-groomed and in possession of great intelligence even after 90 years of life. Robina raised five children and had a Scottish woman's typical skill of multitasking—she was undaunted by any event. Stewart was her firstborn child.

Stewart went to school at Vernon's Mackie Preparatory School and later attended high school in Kamloops. He graduated from the University of British Columbia with a BA and later an MD from McGill. He was determined to finish medical school and served for years in the University Officers Training Corps during World War II until graduating in 1946 with his MD. He started his three-year obstetrical and gynaecological training in Montreal and finished his training in England at the Queen Charlotte's Maternity Hospital and the Chelsea Hospital for Women. Stew married a Vancouverite, Jean Leckie, in London. He passed the certification exam in 1952 and returned to Kamloops to practise medicine.

Stewart was one of the first certified specialists in "Obs and Gyne" in the interior of British Columbia. Stew's affable ways endeared him to all his colleagues. He was well-groomed, like his mother—fit, personable and in possession of impeccable manners. His female patients loved him for his skill and his demeanour.

141

Sterling Haynes

When I practiced midwifery in Williams Lake, he was a beacon. He always returned my emergency telephone calls and helped me and my colleagues with difficult maternity emergency situations in isolated communities.

Stew walked everywhere and he kept fit by playing and winning pairs badminton championships at UBC and McGill University, and later, in the B.C. interior, with his wife, Jean, and singles champion, Bill Dalin, as his partners.

Later in his life, he became a very good squash player. When in his 70's, he ran hard for my drop shot and crashed into the front tin, tearing a hamstring muscle in his leg and cutting his head. I thought he had killed himself at first, but Stew stood up and said, "Maybe I'd better stop playing squash." Stew was a great competitor but the severity of the torn hamstring ended his racquet sports days.

Stewart's hands were strong, his grip sure, his eye keen and his posture excellent. He never tired in the operating room during surgery. He was the fastest and steadiest operator, especially doing caesarean sections, a procedure that I'd never worked with. He'd done close to a thousand in his lifetime and maybe 5000 hysterectomies. Stew delivered 6,107 babies, too. He was a whirlwind in emergencies, whether placenta previa, abruptio, eclampsia and convulsions or locked twins, Stew was the man! I'd never seen him angry or flustered in the operating room with either staff or patients.

Over 40 years ago, the federal laws changed and therapeutic abortion became legal in Canada. The stipulation was that abortions could only be performed where the life or the health of the pregnant woman was in jeopardy. At the Royal Inland Hospital, I served with Douglas Hunter, psychiatrist, and Stew on a committee approving therapeutic abortions for women, provided they were carried out in the Royal Inland Hospital. We seldom turned any woman's request down.

Stewart took a lot of flak over the years from some of his medical colleagues, but mainly from the local pro-life group. This group picketed the hospital and Stewart and Jean's personal residence for years, night and day. Stew never chastised pro-lifers unless they stepped foot on his private property.

Prior to the federal law, I saw a woman with a pelvic infection and a perforated uterus from an illegal abortion gone wrong. Occasionally, in the 1960's, I extracted slippery elm, which had been inserted into the uterus by illegal abortionists in Williams Lake. Once, a hotel room abortionist had shoved lye pellets up the cervical canal of a pregnant woman's uterus. Luckily, with Stewart's phone call and treatment advice to me...the woman lived.

Stew knew his patients. He took a detailed history, especially the family history. Stew knew his patients' families, their backgrounds and even distant relatives. The ranch women were especially enamoured of his knowledge and history of local families. He also knew the history of the area and each ranch or farm in the Thompson and Cariboo regions.

Sixty years ago, when I was practising in Kamloops, one of my maternity patients developed a prolapsed umbilical cord while in hard labour. The unborn child was in foetal distress. I had managed to push the infant back into the pelvis with my gloved right hand, put the mother on oxygen by mask, and move her into the head down position. I called for Stew.

We wheeled the mother to the operating room, which was located one floor up. The elevators were slow and with me under the sheet and pushing the infant's head back and the nurse pushing the gurney, we rushed up to the operating room on the third floor.

While partially concealed under the sheet between floors, I heard a little girl say, "Mommy, what's that man in green overalls doing to that woman having a baby?" Then the elevator door opened and we met Stew, who had run up the stairs and was preparing to scrub for the C-section.

In a matter of minutes, I could feel Stewart's scalpel on my right index finger. I heard Stew say, "The baby boy is out and everything is okay. By the way, was that your finger I cut?"

"Yes, you cut my right glove and index finger. And I may need a couple of stitches."

Stew apologized. Years later, when I see the brand, I am reminded how lucky I was to work with Stew.

At Stewart's retirement party, his colleagues gave him a bronzed corkscrew. This corkscrew was a replica of the large Bonney's corkscrew that he used to screw into a uterus. The handle of the corkscrew was used to pull the uterus out of the pelvis and aid in the dissection of the uterus during a hysterectomy. Stew still has his memento.

Stewart and Jean had three sons. Their eldest, Alan, carries on, in the family tradition, as a general practitioner at the Burris Clinic in Kamloops.

High Maintenance

Six weeks before one Christmas, I started vomiting and couldn't stop. Twenty-four hours later, Jessie trundled me off to the emergency room of Kelowna General Hospital. Dr. Sean and a merry band of nurses managed to stop the vomiting and rehydrated me with intravenous fluid. A small umbilical hernia had grown into a large rupture from the retching. The Norwalk virus was the culprit that caused the vomiting.

My wife and Dr. Sean advised me to see my doctor and I did. Dr. Bernie made an appointment for me to see a general surgeon who advised me to lose weight before surgery. The nurse recommended a weight reduction plan formulated by a group of experts. The receptionist told me that she was going to an international group called Weight Watchers. She gave me their address. The office was in an evangelical church with no elevators.

On Friday the 13th of January, I arrived for the meeting on the second floor of the church. Climbing the long flight of stairs left me puffing as I entered the room. Things looked ominously busy—women talking, being weighed, buying Weight Watchers cookies and books and registering for the course. In addition to all the little kids running around, there were 20 women for each man. I couldn't understand why the majority of women were in attendance. Each of the females looked fit and fashionable. Many of the women's bouffant hairstyles were contoured. I thought, *the higher the hair, the closer to God?*

I soon realized that there was some royalty and religion involved in these meetings. There was a picture of Fergie on the back wall; it was a bit tattered and held to the wall by thumbtacks: their princess and as it turned out—my saviour.

I paid my 12 dollars to receive a booklet of rules, a slide rule for calculating points and calories and my weigh-in card. The trim woman handling the electronic weigh-in scale gasped when she looked at my weight because it was so high. As I plugged in and turned on my hearing aids I heard her ask, "How tall are you?"

"I used to be six-two but I've shrunk in a linear direction by two inches and expanded horizontally."

She looked at me quizzically then said, in a no nonsense way, "Please step over to the receptionist and fill out our admission application form."

The receptionist was a beautiful blonde. She was trim also and wore expensive, form-fitting clothes well. Then I noticed three diamonds on her ring finger. A gold wedding ring was next to her knuckle. The diamond next in line was the smallest, the next two were over one half carat and filled the space to her distal knuckle. She had a sparkling finger to go with her white teeth and radiant smile. I was dazzled.

I wondered to myself how many times she'd been engaged? What could have happened to the first two engaging young men? The old saying entered my brain, *Gentlemen prefer blondes, but do blondes prefer gentlemen?* This receptionist held the answer on her ring finger. Perhaps she had indeed been engaged three times.

The calculated figure for my weight reduction was to be 25 pounds. I was to become a svelte 220 pounds. My goal should to be attained in three months. The calories were estimated by the point system and by using the paper slide rule. It was suggested by our leader and lecturer that we buy food in bulk at Costco. A 100 pound sack of low calorie, crispy, synthetic potato chips was rated best buy of the month. These tough chips were guaranteed to satiate hunger. I wasn't to eat too many. These tasteless potato chips were to last for a year, at least in our household, I would discover. I never returned to replenish my supply.

Our leader was young and personable and presented her pitch with *joie de vivre*. She wore an immaculate pantsuit with a wool shawl that accentuated her figure. The toes of her shoes were pointed and sharp as spearheads, her stiletto three-inch heels were nearly as sharp as her toes. She walked without a wobble.

The next rule suggestion was to use seven-inch plates to serve food. Regular dinner plates, nine inches in diameter, would be better left in the cupboard.

This attractive young woman continued the lesson by giving out silver stars to previous students. Small stars could be attached to your weigh-in book if you lost five pounds. A large star, like a sheriff's badge, could be worn on your sweater if you lost ten pounds.

Over the course of three months, I won two small silver stars for my book. I tried to satiate my hunger by eating the synthetic potato chips. Twice during the three-month course, I lost five pounds in one week. I blushed with the applause and adulation from my female classmates when I went to the front of the class to receive my silver star.

The young beauty, the teacher, had a red streak dyed into her long black hair. Before the start of the first class, I complimented her on the stunning look and suggested that it was similar to the red streak seen on expensive sport cars. I joked that the least her husband could do was to buy her a BMW convertible. Our instructor beamed and she never forgot my first name again.

She began the first lesson with four points written on the white board at the front of the class.

1. Come every week and try to reduce your weight daily.
2. Pay attention.
3. Ask questions and stay focused.

The last rule was...show up every Friday morning.

As a new boy, I was to stay after class with five newcomers of the feminine persuasion for integration and instruction. We were told that while food and calories were important, we *must* drink eight eight-ounce glasses of water per day. Plagued by prostate trouble and a leaking faucet, I thought if I did this I'd have to pick up a jumbo box of adult diapers on my way home.

When we were getting ready to leave, I looked behind me and saw a massive young man with a shaved head and a bearded chin. He must have snuck in quietly. He wore a loose-fitting sweatshirt, same as mine, but his belly appeared slightly bigger. Our combined weight was more than 500 pounds.

On my way out, I was asked to show up next Friday and to buy the latest promotional DVD. "We don't have a player at home for the DVD disc," I replied.

The receptionist shrugged at me and said, "Too bad." She flashed me her radiant smile and sparkling finger. "See you next week."

Tobacco Smoke Enemas

A type of holistic medicine was prominent in London, England in 1774—it was practiced by doctors William Hawes and Thomas Hogan. These two medical practitioners formed The Society for the Recovery of Persons Apparently Drowned. This group later became the The Royal Humane Society and is presently sponsored by Her Majesty, the Queen of England.

The Society promoted the rescue of drowning people and paid four guineas, about 160 dollars in modern currency, to anyone who successfully brought a drowning victim back to life.

During the course of the 18th century, tobacco was imported to England from Virginia to be inhaled, chewed or smoked, usually in a clay pipe, or smouldered as *bum cigars*. American First Nations people have used tobacco as a medicine and pioneered the use of tobacco smoke enemas. The idea of this treatment crossed the water and arrived in England. It was used by volunteer Royal Society medical assistants on London's citizens who were discovered half-drowned before being pulled from the Thames River.

Initially, the pipe smoke London medic inserted an enema tube with rubber tubing attachments into the victim to allow the medic to blow smoke into the rectum. This was erroneously thought—by the medical doctors to do two things—warm the drowned, and secondly, to stimulate respiration.

Sterling Haynes

Artificial respiration was used if the tobacco smoke enema failed.

Soon, tobacco smoke enemas were used for more than just drowning victims. Smoke enemas took a place alongside bloodletting, already in vogue at the time, in the knowledge base of European doctors. They had another gimmick in their bag of medical therapeutic treatments and believed these two miracles of the medical world saved lives.

Now, practitioners had a cure for headaches, respiratory failure, colds, hernias, abdominal cramps—if given with chicken broth concurrently by mouth. Soon, tobacco smoke enemas were used for treating typhoid fever and even cholera outbreaks during the stage of collapse and death.

Before bellows were included in the resuscitation kit, the results could be disastrous to the tobacco smoke blower. If the practitioner or medic inadvertently sucked up instead of blowing out, or into, during a coughing spell, some rice water stools of the cholera flagellates could be aspirated and swallowed. His demise would be due to a cough, dehydration and diarrhoea. It was not always swift either.

With the advent of bellows and a variety of rectal tubes, the medics were spared from these infectious scourges. The practice, along with leeches, turpentine stoops for haemorrhoids and carbuncles, was judged to be medically sound during that era.

In 1811, English scientist Ben Brodie discovered that nicotine was toxic to the heart. Soon it wasn't so fashionable to prescribe tobacco smoke enemas. The kits along with lancets and phlebotomies were soon easily purchased in London's second-hand stores, as well as pawn and charity shops. Perhaps a posting now would read:

To those I can only question as sadomasochists, who are presently addicted to tobacco smoke enemas, and do want treatment, I would prescribe nicotine patches. This may or may not help them to kick their smoking habit with enemas.

If you are interested in purchasing such an antique kit, you might try:

Dr. Manly Bracegirdle,
Ye Olde English Medical Implement Shoppe,
Water Street, Wretched Mess, MA, USA, 12345.

There are shortages. So please, don't hold your breath.

Sterling Haynes

Popping the Cork

In 1817, Shuswap Indian Chief Littleleg's skull was trepanned, or bored, by his friends on the bank of the upper reaches of Jacques Creek in the Okanagan Valley of British Columbia. The chief had been tracking a bear along the creek when the bear attacked him, scalped him and fractured his skull. He lay unconscious until his native friends found him and drove the bear off. They were armed with muskets and each warrior carried a *gun worme*. With their gun wormes, they successfully trepanned Chief Littleleg's skull, dealt with the fractures, then sewed his scalp back on with animal sinew.

The gun worme is a long metal corkscrew used to clean the barrel of muskets or extract unspent charges from gun barrels. The worme, or corkscrew, has been used by primitive people to drill holes in the bony part of the skull after people lose consciousness. Sometimes the screw can also be inserted into the bone and the depressed skull fracture pulled out—much like popping a cork from a bottle.

The original creator of the corkscrew was Reverend Samuel Henshall of Middlesex, England. In 1795, he patented the corkscrew to easily remove corks from hundreds of blessed wine bottles. He likely popped many a cork, both for church services and pleasurable wine tasting by the clergy. A few years later, a type of corkscrew was developed for use in muskets, a prototype of the gun worme.

Small, round holes drilled in the skull are now called burr holes. This technique is still used successfully by neurosurgeons to control bleeding under the skull and evacuate blood clots in cases of epidural and subdural traumatic bleeds. The procedure has been used for centuries by primitive tribes worldwide. Skulls excavated by archaeologists in Meso-America show neat round holes. A few cases of trepanation have been found in skulls in more modern indigenous burial sites in America as well.

The explorer and writer Alexander Ross in his book *Fur Traders of the Far West,* printed 150 years ago, recorded the fact that trepanning of the skull took place on or near Okanagan Lake. Leonard Norris, an early historian from Peachland, claims that Jacques Creek was renamed Trepanier Creek in the 19th century to commemorate the trepanning of Chief Littleleg's skull. Norris relates the following story:

The name Trepanier Creek had something to do with 'trepanning', the surgical operation of removing a piece of bone from the skull, or the instrument used in doing so.

So, if you are visiting Trepanier Creek, formerly Jacques Creek, in Peachland, during the fall season, you can watch the Kokanee spawning and visit the many Okanagan wineries. But after extensive wine tasting, let's say popping the cork, please keep an eye out for the ghost of Chief Littlelegs.

It has been said that in the rising mist of Lake Okanagan, at the mouth of Trepanier Creek, if you focus real hard and drill your vision into the mist, you just may see a short native figure with a circular scar at the base of his scalp, a musket in his right hand, a gun worme in his left.

Sterling Haynes

The Carbolic Smoke Ball Company

Many law students worldwide study a medical treatment that was prevalent around flu season, a long time ago. The treatment was called a carbolic smoke ball that was reportedly used to prevent the Russian flu during the epidemic seasons of 1889 and 1890 in England.

Tobacco smoke enemas were no longer in vogue and bleeding and purging the sick was on the wane. What was a doctor to prescribe over 100 years ago? Doctors and pharmacists combined with a great public health measure developed by the Carbolic Smoke Ball Company. This company developed a rubber ball that enclosed powdered carbolic acid (phenol), to be used three times a day for two weeks and was advertised to prevent the flu.

A smoke ball was a container filled with phenol that had a tube attached to it. The tube was run up the nose and the powdered carbolic acid would be released somewhere in the oro-nasal passages at the end of the tube. Just one puff did the trick.

The company, in 1892, stated that the carbolic smoke ball puff would positively cure "colds in the head, colds in the chest, coughs, asthma, catarrh, loss of voice, sore throat, treat deafness, snoring, sore eyes, influenza, headache, croup, whooping cough and neuralgia."

In an advertisement in the *Pall Mall Gazette*, the Carbolic Smoke Company offered a 100 pound Sterling reward given from their Alliance Bank account to anyone who "used the ball correctly and then contracted influenza."

The lairds, clergy and aristocrats endorsed the treatment—it became fashionable. Sales went up for the carbolic smoke ball until Mrs. Louisa Elizabeth Carlill claimed the 100 pound Sterling reward. Louisa Elizabeth "bought the ball and used it three times a day for almost two months, then promptly caught the flu." The medical pundits thought that the puff' of toxic phenol would run cold out the nose and the infection would be "flushed out."

Louisa's husband was an English solicitor and after two letters requesting the reward, the Carlills sued the company. The Carbolic Smoke Ball Company claimed "she would have to attend their office on 27 Princess Street, Hanover Square, London each day and have their secretary use the toxic phenol flush up her nose." Elizabeth Louisa refused the company's "flush puff" and sued.

The company went to the Appellate Court (Civil Division) and that decision is now on law books in countries around the world: It is a classical introductory contract case and is studied by freshmen law students today worldwide. Mrs. Carlill won her case in the high court. All three English judges were unanimous in their decision to award the 100 pounds to Louisa. At last, under English law the consumer was protected.

Carbolic acid or phenol is, and was, very inexpensive and has been used as an antiseptic in carbolic acid soap, hair colourings, sunscreens, combined with lipsyls, skin lightening preparations and chloraseptic gargles. Inhalation of phenol vapour may cause oedema of the lung. During World War II, Zyklon-B (cyanide) pellets were used by the Nazis to exterminate Jews in the gas chambers in Auschwitz. Later, for smaller groups of Jews, it was cheaper to inject one gram of phenol into their veins to kill them. In Islay Scotch whiskey, phenol in 30-150 parts per million has been used to provide the distinctive aroma and taste.

This Carlill legal case helped ordinary people fight large companies. In Europe, for example, the use of thalidomide was used to stop the nausea and vomiting of pregnancy until 1961 with disastrous results on the newborn.

Dr. Francis Kelsey stopped the sale of thalidomide in the U.S. and western Canada, you may remember from my previous story about her life. However, she was also vilified by the large corporations of the pharmaceutical companies. Dr. Kelsey's continued work was responsible, in part, for the U.K.'s Medicines Act of 1968 and the Trade Descriptions Act. These acts spelled out consumers rights and the rights of the unborn child in Europe. Large companies were thwarted from continuing to damage unborn children with the help of the Carlill versus carbolic smoke ball case.

Louisa Elizabeth Carlill died in 1942 at the age of 96. Her name is on the law books for challenging companies and protecting consumer rights.

Her English physician signed her death certificate's cause of death as: "Old Age and Influenza."

A spring-loaded lancet circa 1760's—another medical device with dire results. This sort of device was used to drain President George Washington of up to seven pints of blood, leading to his untimely demise after suffering from a sore throat.

Ethermaniacs

Almost 60 years ago when I started a rural medical practice in Williams Lake, I found some of my patients were using Hoffman's Drops, consisting of one part ether to three parts alcohol, for different ills. The first usage of these drops was by Canadian-Russian prairie women who, 100 years ago, used them for menstrual cramps. Soon the drops became common in Canadian rural medicine cabinets. The drops could be obtained from a non-medical mail order supplier in Winnipeg.

Sterling Haynes

As a general practitioner and anaesthetist in the Williams Lake Cariboo Memorial Hospital, I used di-ethyl open drop ether to put people to sleep. The older docs sometimes used "one, two, three," a mixture of chloroform (one part), ether (two parts) and alcohol (three parts) which was dropped over a gauze-lined Schimmelbusch metal mask. All these agents could be toxic, though I found ether to be a very safe anaesthetic agent when mixed with nitrous oxide and oxygen. The common name for ether is sweet vitriol and ether, combined with alcohol; it gave the user a sweet *buzz*. One of the early ether pioneers was Oliver Wendell Holmes. In 1870, Holmes gave the Phi Beta Kappa address to the fellows of Harvard University on his thoughts and morals of sweet vitriol. He related how he experimented with ether vapour:

The mighty music of the triumphal march into nothingness reverberated through my brain, and filled me with a sense of infinite possibilities, which made me an archangel for a moment. The veil of eternity was lifted. The one great truth which underlies all human experiences and is the key to all the mysteries that philosophy has sought in vain to solve, flashed upon me in a sudden revelation. Henceforth all was clear: a few words had lifted my intelligence to the level of the knowledge of a cherub.

"The veil of eternity" was never lifted for ethermaniacs like Holmes. The addiction spread across the world.

Miners in south eastern Poland mixed ether with coffee or raspberry juice. In 1928, Poland forbade the sale of ether in bars and pharmacies. The use of ether was common in England from 1850 until 1930. It was used by the gentry as well as the blue collar workers in the farms and mines. Among the upper classes, a cocktail martini consisting of a cut strawberry impregnated with two or three drops of ether covered by champagne was popular.

158

Three or four of these drinks could reduce you to a childlike idiot, living in an ethereal, personal paradise.

Ether drinking was also common in Ireland. Dr. Kelly's Remedy, "strong ether," was in big demand as it was said to produce a "blithesome gladness."

The dangers of explosions and fire with ether use are very real. Ether-induced eruptions while smoking could be catastrophic.

Despite the dangers, a Bellaghy man from the county of Londonderry wrote about the pleasures of combining ether and tobacco: "I knew a man that was always drinkin' it and won day after a dose uv it, he wint to light his pipe and the fire cot his breath and tuk fire inside." The man's life was saved when the bartender poured a jug of water down his throat.

Some of Canada's Russian, Ukrainian and Polish immigrants brought Hoffman's Drops to farms in the western provinces. As well as relieving cramps, they dulled the pain of common injuries such as fractures. Ether was used where there were few doctors. But it was an addictive cure-all.

I left Williams Lake in 1966. I haven't given any ether anaesthetics nor had I heard about ether addiction until I heard of the book *Fear and Loathing in Las Vegas* written by author, and addict, Hunter S. Thompson.

Thompson writes about "grass, mescaline, a saltshaker half full of cocaine, uppers, downers, screamers, laughers, tequila, rum, a case of beer, a pint of raw ether and a dozen amyls." Thompson urged people to "buy the ticket, take the ride," as he did. But he was cautious about ether.

Sterling Haynes

The only thing that really worried me was ether, he wrote. *There is nothing in the world more helpless, irresponsible and depraved than a man in the depths of an ether binge and I knew we'd get into that rotten stuff pretty soon.*

I don't know if Hoffman's Drops are still being produced. But I do know that the American dream is still clouded by the vapours of toxic ether.

Works cited in this essay are from:

Oliver Wendell Holmes, *Mechanism in Thought and Morals.* Phi Beta Kappa address, Harvard University, June 29th, 1870 (Boston: J.R. Osgood and Company, 1871)

William (August13, 1910), *Ether Drinking in Ulster, British Medical Journal 2* (2589): 387-389

Hunter S. Thompson (1972), *Fear and Loathing in Las Vegas: A Savage Journey to the Heart of the American Dream.* The lines quoted were spoken in the 1998 movie of the same name starring Johnny Depp.

Writing Funny

Comedienne Lilly Tomlin had a great one-liner: "No matter how cynical you become, it's never enough."

Writing funny can be difficult for an 85-year-old writer, a retired doc. The difficulty can be due to motor failure and faulty brakes, as my humour and satire lose horsepower. Perhaps I'm grinding to a halt. Is that my clutch slipping? Or has my power failed and gaskets blown, leaving patches of oil scattered on my blank highway of pages passed?

Great lines don't come so easily now and I have to detour, re-enter the idea or thought to try and make it laughable. After I had a stroke 15 years ago, I became aphasic and had a paralyzed right foot. My brain recovered and found a solution—words went through a maze and I did communicate in an offbeat way. My right foot remains paralyzed, but my brain, until recently, worked well in a humorous vein. Generally, I know I got the better of the deal. Until now.

The gray matter is still working and I am writing, but the gears shift slowly, so slowly that when I try to remember recent incidents and time periods—there are gaps, slippage. Under the guidance of my alter ego and close associate, Al Zeimer from Biggar, Saskatchewan, I try to see the big sky and big picture. However, the emptiness of Al and vastness of my unconnected ideas cloud up and it starts to rain in my head.

Al is a close companion some of the time. A sun shower dampens my dusty thoughts and prairie winds buffer my synapses, and then I can't remember. Internal lightning and the electrical storms short circuit words and I lose the thread of the conversation on my pages.

My docs tell me, "You're just getting old," but I know deep in my heart that "getting old" is a diagnosis that doesn't get any better. They don't have the cure or pill for me. My 5000 dollar hearing aids offer a little solace. Mostly, I can hear now, that is, when I remember to turn them on. My docs tell me I'm aging and getting an attitude problem, besides—well, that's their problem, right?

These same docs have been good to me though. I couldn't walk a block and my right knee froze up a couple of years ago in the heat of summer—it wouldn't bend. They found a way to saw off my leg bone and thighbone in order to hammer in a new titanium knee. They used crazy glue to cement it in. I could smell the epoxy cement in the Kelowna General Hospital surgery recovery room. They said that they used a tube full, but it wouldn't have any lasting effects on my brain. Sometimes I wonder if I'm stuck with some after effects? You've read my book, you can be the judge. I just don't have time for worrying. Oops, there's my attitude showing.

Yes, for awhile the knee was *a big ouch*, but I did rehab and *the ouch* got better. Those strong Amazonian physiotherapists get you going fast. Their mantra is "no pain, no gain." I am a living believer, well, so far anyway! Now when I get up, I remember their other mantra, "Nose over toes and push yourself up out of the chair with your arms."

The bone doc said my new knee could last 15 years. For some reason, he didn't make a follow up appointment with me for 2025...hmmm.

A few months ago, another doctor said I had "a big balloon of an abdominal aortic aneurysm ready to burst." They made scans, took measurements, and sent them to the Mississauga factory to make me a customized new stent for my aorta. These good people in Ontario made it fast and shipped it west to my doc by UPS. Why not Canada Post, you ask—it wasn't fast enough. Canada Post might go the way of the dodo before I do anyway, right?

Anyway, this stent was made of Gore-Tex and stainless steel. It's strong and does not leak. It's guaranteed in wet weather. The vascular surgeon, who put it in, said it was "good for 15 years." When I get to be 100 years of age, it may start to break down. Maybe?

My body may have reached my deadline then—unless something else *happy* happens to me. I'll keep my fingers crossed and try to remember.

The number 100 is hard to forget, isn't it?

Sterling Haynes

Acknowledgements

I would like to thank my family, the women in my life, who helped me with this collection of stories. Jessie, Elizabeth and Leslie were instrumental in getting me started writing. Elizabeth and Leslie edited my work and corrected my mistakes. Elizabeth edited all of these stories and made suggestions. Melissa and Jocelyn promoted my work. Dona Sturmanis, my first teacher of creative writing outside the home, also did a final proofreading of this book.

Rand Zacharias did the final editing and publishing. I thank him. I am also indebted to Bill Richardson for teaching me how to write humour and Fred Stenson on how to construct a story and write for magazines.

Sage Birchwater's collection of photographs of First Nations people was excellent. Also, I want to thank everyone who helped me and supplied pictures for this book, especially Charlotte Falk, architect and artist, who created the cover. Her portrait of my mother, Elizabeth, her great grandmother, is outstanding. Thank you, Charlotte.

About The Author

Haynes embraces his grandchildren, Carson on his right, Rachel on his left.

Sterling Haynes is an octogenarian writer. His first book, *Bloody Practice*, published by Caitlin Press, was a bestseller in his home province of British Columbia. His second book, *Wake-Up Call*, is now available as an eBook.

In 2008, Haynes won the French Naji Naaman Literary Prize and later the Joyce Dunn Award in B.C. for creative non-fiction. In 2013, the Arts Council of the Okanagan awarded him a magnificent glass statue for excellence in the Literary Arts.

His stories and poetry have appeared in Canadian anthologies and magazines including *The New Quarterly, The Medical Post, The BC Medical Journal, The Rocky Mountain Goat, The Canadian Journal of Rural Medicine* and *Haiku Canada.*

CPSIA information can be obtained at www.ICGtesting.com
Printed in the USA
LVOW10s1506260914

406067LV00002B/346/P